A Different World

A Different World

An English Vicar
in West Cork

Hilary Wakeman

The Liffey Press

Published by
The Liffey Press Ltd
'Clareville', 307 Clontarf Road
Dublin D03 PO46, Ireland
www.theliffeypress.com

© 2021 Hilary Wakeman

A catalogue record of this book is
available from the British Library.

ISBN 978-1-8383593-5-5

Photos of the author on the front cover, page viii
and page 154 by John Minihan

Drawings on pages 77 and 79 by Brian Lalor

Printed in Spain by GraphyCems

Contents

Acknowledgements   *vi*

Dedication   *vii*

Foreword   1

Spring 1996   5

Summer 1996   56

Autumn 1996   87

Winter 1997   122

Spring 1997   143

Afterword   165

Acknowledgements

Thanks to family and friends who read the original diary by installments, encouraging its continuance. To Canon Paul Willoughby and Rose Briscoe for fact-checking and advice. To Catherine, and to David.

Thanks to the people of the parish, for all their kindness during our time there, and for my having been allowed to be part of their lives.

Dedication

To our beloved daughter
Rhiannon ('Rosie') Apple Edith Shelley
(1970–2019)

How It All Began

I guess it is not unusual if you have a good holiday to dream of moving there.

In the spring of 1995 my husband John and I took a week's holiday in Ireland. We had been to Dublin a couple of times, but never seen any of the rest of the country, or the people from whom I liked to think I was descended. So we went to the west coast of Ireland, to Co. Clare. We took my elderly Irish mother with us, and our 25-year-old daughter Rosie Rhiannon came too. Our cottage was good, the people were great, and the traditional Irish music in the pubs was mind-blowingly wonderful. But it rained all week. We had so looked forward to seeing the amazing rock landscape of the Burren but what with the rain, and my mother being less mobile than we had realised, we saw very little of it. And Rosie, who had just broken up with her partner, was depressed. So you could say it was not the best ever holiday.

1

Driving back down to the Cork ferry we diverted into one of the many peninsulas of the southwest of Ireland, and found the fishing village of Castletownbeare. It was sunny, and pleasant, and friendly. And then I saw the Church of Ireland church there. It was clearly not in use, but what distressed me was that there was a great lashing of chains and padlock on the high iron gates. Keep out, it seemed to say.

When we got back home to Norwich I couldn't get that church out of my mind. Was there a vacancy? What would it be like to work there?

The Church of Ireland had begun ordaining women as priests in 1990. Four years later the Church of England followed suit. As an Established Church it had not only had to get the agreement of its General Synod but also of Parliament. I had been one of the first 800 women to be ordained priest in the Church of England in 1994, and was now the vicar of a city centre church in Norwich. Ecumenism, the possible coming together of the various Christian churches and denominations, had been of real importance to me for a long time. Clearly, with the Church of England being an Established Church it would be a very long time before anything like that would happen. But the Church of Ireland is not established. From a variety of things I had read it seemed possible that full ecumenism might become a reality in Ireland. How marvellous it would be to be there, part of it when it happened.

The day after we got back to Norwich I took John to our local pub, bought him a pint and said, 'How would you feel about moving to Ireland?' I explained how I was thinking.

'Why not?' he said. He was a freelance writer and editor so he could work from anywhere.

I wrote to the Diocesan Secretary of the Diocese of Cork, Cloyne & Ross, and asked if there was a vacancy in Castletownbeare. No, an appointment had just been made. That was a downer. Six months later, in March 1996, there was a vacancy further south, based in another fishing village. I applied, was shortlisted, and the Bishop asked me to come over for interviews the next week, bringing John. I was interviewed formally by the Bishop, and then, seriously but very enjoyably, by the Dean of Cork and several others. Seventy miles further west we were shown the parish by the four kindly and impressive parish Nominators. I was accepted.

Planning our move west

We were moving to Ireland.

Already we knew it was going to be a very different world. So I decided to keep a diary, to send to the family and friends we would be leaving behind. This, with some amendments and some names removed or changed, is it.

CHURCH ■ Anglican woman priest leaves city for the wild countryside of Co Cork

The local media found our move newsworthy

Spring 1996

April 20 – Saturday – Norwich

Two and a half weeks to moving day, and we heard last night that the Rectory is not going to be ready to move into when we arrive. A phone call from Nan, one of the Nominators who showed us the parish in March, and our most regular contact with the parish. The church authorities have upgraded Rectory standards, she says. So ours has to have a new concrete floor, and double glazing, as well as the central heating that had been agreed on. We will have to go into temporary accommodation for what Nan guessed would be about three or four weeks. Fortunately she has a cottage that she lets out to summer visitors. Where will our furniture go, and our books and piano? In the Rectory outbuildings, Nan says.

April 24 – Wednesday

A friend has sent us a couple of copies of a rural Cork local paper. It really is a different world. All the people in all the photographs stand or sit looking straight forward at the camera, smiling unselfconsciously. No clever camera angles, no clever lenses. I am torn between impatience at the old-fashionedness of it – how many decades is it since English newspapers were like that? – and wanting nothing to alter such an absence of sophistication.

April 28 – Sunday

My last day at St George Colegate – a 'sad and proud day' as it says in the prayers I often use at funerals. But – as I also often say at funerals – the people I have known and loved here will always be a part of me now. (And maybe I will still be a part of them.)

I can't quite believe I'm leaving it. I'm remembering back to 1989, when Michael Archdeacon of Norwich came to St Thomas's in the inner suburbs, where I had been a curate for nearly five years, to ask me how I would feel about being Deacon-in-Charge of St George Colegate, the beautiful large city centre church with huge clear windows. How could I be in charge of a parish, when I wasn't yet a priest because the Church of England was still wrestling with the idea of the ordination of women? The Archdeacon said that two priests from neighbouring parishes, and some retired clergy, would help with the services. And I'm remembering my installation when Bishop Peter said to the congregation, 'The lawyers will tell you Hilary is the Deacon-in-Charge, but I tell you she's your Vicar.'

And I'm remembering the next few years, as the churchwardens and the Parochial Church Council and Mary the Parish Worker and I struggled to make something of what someone had once said was the second most run down parish in the city. The church has a most wonderful George English organ of 1802 – but there was then no organist. A short while after I began work there I was saying Morning Prayer, alone, in the church one day, and found myself actually begging for an organist. When I finished and stood up I realise someone had slipped in to the back of the church and was sitting quietly. I went to her. 'Would it be possible for me to play the organ sometimes?' she said. That was Anne, and she has been the most splendid organist from that day to this.

We put on a series of free lectures, one a week for about nine weeks, on serious social and theological topics given by well-known writers and academics, lay people or clergy, local or from places like London or Cambridge. Three more series followed.

Some former Hell's Angels, now the Christian Motorcyclists Union, came to ask if they could use the church for their weekly home-made service and we said a delighted Yes. One of them, Jingles, became one of our churchwardens. I was so proud of him – and us – when at the annual diocesan admission of churchwardens in the cathedral, Jingles walked forward, in leathers and tattoos, with our other very proper middle-aged churchwarden.

We were also the meeting place for a time of the Norwich branch of the Lesbian and Gay Christian Movement, founded by a Methodist woman minister and me.

When one Sunday the roof started to drop small lumps of rubble we closed the building, started a funding appeal, and used St Clement's along the road for several months. And had a joyful service when we went back in to St George's again, albeit with quite a large debt still hanging over us.

I wonder if I will one day think 'What have I done? Why did I ever leave that wonderful church and those much-loved people?' – The Church of Ireland is going to be a very different place.

May 4 – Saturday

The furniture is all taken away from our large, gaunt three-storey house in Norwich. All except mattresses, a few chairs, the kettle and a cup and plate for each of us to use for the next three days – because we have by chance chosen a bank holiday weekend for our move. Pickfords will come back very early on Tuesday for these last things, and go off across England and Wales to Swansea for the night ferry. John and Rosie and I will follow, stopping to visit my mother in South Wales.

But meanwhile we live for three days in the strangeness of this empty house that is still, and yet isn't, home. 'Home' doesn't exist anymore. It's not in Pickfords' van, even though those pieces of furniture, those books and pictures, are part of what makes it. Such a basic, primitive desire, that longing to 'go home.' The tragedy of homelessness is not just the absence of a roof over a person's head.

May 6 – Monday

Saying goodbye to the family has been far more painful than I had anticipated. I remember our parents saying goodbye to John and me when we got married in 1957 and went off that very day to start our journey to America.

For all they knew we would never return. And there were no cheap transatlantic phone calls in those days, much less cheap transatlantic flights. And then I remember my mother's Irish family, and all the Irish parents who must have stood on quaysides seeing off their children to America, almost certainly never to see them again; and the terrible heartache of that.

May 7 – Tuesday

Across England and Wales, stopping to see my family. Then on to the night ferry at Swansea.

May 8 – Wednesday – Ireland

Through the summer morning mist, the low green coast of Cork. Then a hard bright sun breaks through as we move into the harbour. The words 'the land of saints and scholars' come to me. The anxieties that have been pressing in for some days suddenly lift.

We arrived at the Rectory just after 9.00 am yesterday. We had driven through part of Cork city, and the towns of Bandon, Clonakilty, Skibbereen, and then the very small town which is virtually the beginning of our new parish, and the only town in it. The parish is the whole peninsula and is about fifteen miles long, and varying between two and six miles wide. The town has the largest of the three churches. Five miles further west is the Rectory and a small church. There is a village a few miles further and then, at the very end of the peninsula, an even smaller village and the smallest church of all.

The landscape – hills, sea, gorse, rock, grass and vigorous plants of considerable variety – is amazing,

The amazing local landscape

beautiful, all that I have ever dreamt about. And everywhere there are cows and sheep. I think I had not really taken it all in during our one brief visit here for the interviews. Doubtless I was concentrating on the conversations with the four parish Nominators who were showing us around.

We arrived at the Rectory before the Pickfords van. From the brief look John and I had had of the house at the interview we knew that it was fairly isolated, apart from the small church and one holiday bungalow. All three are set behind a low curved sea wall with a rocky cove the other side of it.

The narrowness of the entrance to the Rectory drive was, however, something else we had not noticed or remembered. We had assured the removals men there would be no trouble with access. Now clearly there was. We were there before the van, and John was dreadfully worried about it all during the time we waited for them. Would the long van be able to take all those curves, especially the sharp turn from the road into the drive? We walked up the drive (later we discovered it is called 'the avenue') to the house, and found it full of cheerful builders, with the floors up and, as Rosie said, the walls down. In some places the interior walls were stripped of plaster so that what showed was a construction that looked unnervingly like a drystone wall. The whole downstairs was chaotic, but the upstairs had been done: raw grey plaster surrounds the new double-glazed windows. We went back down the drive and sat on the low stone wall by the sea, near the gateway, in the sunshine, and I tried to realise that we were really here, that this was now the surroundings of our new life.

Our first re-meeting with Nan was with a hug and a kiss, and the same from Betty, one of the other Nominators. We were invited a short stretch up the road to Nan's for a cup of coffee. She runs the local shop – hardly a 'village shop' as there are only a handful of houses there – and Post Office. She owns the cottage we are to stay in, opposite the Post Office and the green mail box and the green phone booth.

The cup of coffee turned out to be quite a social occasion. Eight or so parishioners had been invited in to meet us, and stood in a rather shy circle in the small old-fashioned living room behind the shop and there were introductions all round, with many fairly formal words of welcome, each slightly different, but all basically

Two views of the Rectory when we first arrived

'Welcome to West Cork.' Until then we hadn't known that this part of County Cork was known as West Cork. Coffee was not just coffee but big plates of brack bread and a sort of fruity cake. More people kept turning up to be introduced and be found a seat and given coffee. I thought it all wonderful. But I could see why Rosie was rather overwhelmed by it all.

Eventually we were told the removal van had arrived, and John's anxieties about access were well founded. After some very skilful attempts at backing and turning to try to get the van to turn from the road into the gateway, our excellent driver Ken had to give up. 'These things happen,' was the reassuring comment of one of the two extra moving men whom Ken had collected from Cork. A local man with a pick-up truck was brought in, with two lads, to ferry the furniture and packing boxes from the layby by the sea wall, up the two hundred yard long drive to the house. Filing cabinets had to be dismantled, and chests of drawers had their drawers of clothing carried independently of their chests.

Because of the necessity of getting Ken and the van back to Cork in time for the night ferry – if the diocese is not to get an increased bill – John and I pitched in with the unloading from the truck into the house, as did Billy, another of the parish Nominators. Ken didn't object, as I'm sure he would normally have done on grounds of insurance. It was startling to see him literally run up the stairs carrying loads that most men would find it a challenge simply to walk with.

It took all day. We paused only at midday to go up the road to Nan's for plates and plates of sandwiches and cups and cups of tea. For most of the day the Rectory was flooded with sunshine, and we got a strong sense of what a lovely house it is going to be to live in. Mid-nineteenth century, with five bedrooms and three reception rooms not counting the porch-room. Between truck loads we wandered about, falling in love with the garden and its possibilities – the lawn is more than big enough to

The avenue the removal van couldn't negotiate

have a tennis lawn – but failing to find the vegetable garden that is said to be somewhere behind the house. There is nowhere that it can be, as beyond the long lawn everything seems to be rock. We think the vegetable garden is a myth.

Everywhere is crowded with small white flowers, tall and delicate, that at first we took to be a sort of white bluebell. It was only when we asked one of the moving men about the herby smell in the air that we learned that the prolific white flower is wild garlic.

We finished at about 6.30 pm, saw Ken off, and went back to the pleasant little traditional cottage where we will be living for the next few weeks. Supper consisted of champagne and chocolates given to us by my sister just before we left Wales; and bread, lettuce and tomatoes that Nan had laid in for us along with milk and butter and tea; and wonderful cold roast chicken, and homemade apple pie and cream brought round by Jenny, another parishioner. We tried to watch television but were too tired to follow anything, and all three of us went to bed early.

In a year's time the smell of wild garlic will bring this amazing day back to us.

May 9 – Thursday

Have just been telephone-interviewed by RTÉ radio, though I wasn't clear what the angle was. I know I'm not the first clergy woman in Ireland to be in charge of a parish, as there are two others somewhere. First woman Rector in this diocese, presumably. We have no phone at the cottage here, so I arranged to take the call at 3.00 pm at the public phone box outside Nan's Post Office, but just as I was crossing the road at 2.55 pm a huge concrete mixer drew up and the driver went into the phone box and started a long conversation. RTÉ took the initiative of dialling Nan's number, and she came out to get me.

May 10 – Friday

My institution as Rector is this evening. It will be in the largest church of the three, the one in the small town. Yesterday evening we had a rehearsal in the church. I was surprised and pleased to find that I already know by name most of the two dozen or so people who were gathered there.

A letter has arrived from the Bishop of Norwich, saying that Honorary Canons of Norwich Cathedral normally vacate office on leaving the diocese. He would therefore like to appoint me an Honorary Canon Emeritus, retaining the title for life. My new parishioners seem ecstatic, and someone has rushed off to get someone to re-paint my name on the newly painted noticeboards.

Paul, the Rector of a neighbouring parish (all incumbents are Rectors here, no Vicars) has been doing most of the service taking and home visits since my predecessor left about three months ago. He ran the rehearsal in a pleasantly relaxed manner, and smoothed the way through some upset that suddenly flared up. I caught the first whiff of rivalries and umbrage-taking among some of the office-holding parishioners. Before the evening was over I was in possession of enough facts to know that there will be a few problems. Going to one of the village pubs afterwards with Paul and two of the younger women who are office-holding parishioners was very enjoyable, but tinged with the slight worry of being seen to be taking sides.

At the rehearsal one of the women – small, elderly – seemed to be standing by herself. I went to talk to her. She beamed, and took my hand. 'Welcome, welcome,' she said. 'You don't look a bit like your picture in the paper.' Was that a good or a bad thing, I wondered. 'But you are welcome all the same,' she said. 'You are welcome all the same.'

May 11 – Saturday

The service of institution was fine. Bishop Roy, who had been my main interviewer two months ago, is a dear, and the church interior was wonderfully pink and lighted and warm and flowery. ('I've never seen a pink church before,' said Rosie.) By 8.00 pm the building was full – about 250 people. The service went reasonably well, though I missed the sense of style with which Norwich diocese does such things. All sorts and conditions of people came up during the Welcome, including the two local Catholic priests and some nuns, the local librarian, the TD (local member of the national government), the bank manager, the undertaker, the garda (policeman), the matron of the town hospital, and so on. That was really good. After the service there were 250 handshakes at the door, 'Welcome!' they said, one after another: the young, the old, the lively, the confused, but nearly all with such beautiful smiles. After various posings in various groups for the local freelance photographer, we all went down the road to the Community College for 'the bash'. A huge table full of sandwiches and homemade cakes and cups of tea and a hallful of people and eventually some speeches. I met so many people, and nearly every name was told to me, so that my earlier success with remembering names was quite lost.

John and Rosie and I went back to the cottage in the still-warm darkness, amazed to find that it was eleven o'clock.

May 12 – Sunday

My first two services today, both Holy Communion. Ten o'clock in the town church where the installation had been last night, and 11.30 am in the country church next to the Rectory. Forty-plus people at each. Odd to think that it was these services that had given me the most anxiety in the days leading up to the move. Largely, I think, because the wording of the services used by the Church of Ireland are all slightly different to what I had been accustomed to in the Church of England. But when it came, the whole day was quite without anxiety, only pleasant anticipation.

After the service in the town church, one of the parishioners, backed by another, expressed a worry that I wore a white cassock alb for a Communion service. There were certainly no high church vestments in evidence, so that seemed to me the obvious apparel.

'Why wouldn't I?' I asked.

Indignantly, she said, 'Because that's what *they* wear.'

'They' meant the Catholics. The parishoners thought I should wear a black cassock with a white surplice over it, plus a coloured stole. And they thought I shouldn't make a large sign of the cross over the congregation at the final blessing. For the same reason. I expect they will get used to both things, if they are happy enough with everything else.

I suspect my brief sermons need to be even briefer. When I left the town church I had just ten minutes to drive the five miles to the other one – and met a herd of cows in the road. A very long line of them. 'The congregation will wait,' I told myself. 'I can't do anything about this.' But then the cows moved into the left-hand side of the road, giving me space to drive slowly along beside them.

After lunch John and Rosie and I went for a drive around the end of the peninsula. There wasn't much petrol in the car, and where do you get petrol in the middle of the country on a Sunday? Looking at the map, it seemed possible to go left and then keep going left at every turn, so that we could see the coast on the north side of the peninsula and arrive back where we started on the coast on the south side. Something went wrong. But if we missed the lanes we should have taken it can only be that they didn't look like lanes. Perhaps we assumed they were just tracks up to farms and houses and cottages. We went almost to the end of the peninsula, saw some more incredibly beautiful scenery, worried about the petrol – and ended up in a small village with a homely pub that sold petrol.

This evening I was called out to see an elderly parishioner in a nursing home, said to be going downhill fast, probably dying. When I arrived she was sitting up cheerfully in bed. We had a lively chat, said a prayer, and I promised to take Holy Communion to her next Thursday. I shall perhaps be slower to believe such drama next time. But she was a lovely woman and I didn't regret the call. The evening sun was wonderful on the way back, the more so because after Friday evening the weather has deteriorated, and today has been rainy. This evening the sea and the hills were fresh and bright and golden.

May 13 – Monday

The wild flowers are gorgeous. As well as the white wild garlic flowers everywhere there are great swathes of primroses in some places and, when you look carefully, wild violets in the grass and hedgerows. Also, huge patches of almost purple bluebells and in the graveyard of the country church there are a great many reddish-purple flowers that none of us recognised until we were told: it was the early purple orchid.

Two views of Nan's cottage

There are many magpies about, far more than we are used to seeing. And lots of pied wagtails. We heard the cuckoo on our second day here, and most days since then. We often see a robin in the front garden of this cottage where we are staying, but the other day John called us to look quickly at the gate. There on the two white gateposts were two robins, posed like tiny heraldic creatures , each facing the cottage.

Finding things – not just books but cooking equipment, office things, specific clothes – among the great stacks of boxes upstairs in the Rectory is not easy. We are very much camping here in Nan's cottage. The three of us take turns to do the cooking. But lacking kitchen scales or measuring cups, we guess amounts of ingredients, and today I rolled out pastry with a wine bottle. More seriously, we are finding food in particular quite expensive, and anything at all exotic is unavailable. I find myself reverting to a way of thinking that was natural to us when our first four children were babies and we were very poor. It is not unpleasant: a packet of biscuits becomes a real pleasure instead of something you buy without thinking. I guess our lives will not be desperately diminished by the lack of sun-dried tomatoes and basmati rice and avocados. Wine is oddly expensive, with no cheap plonk, which is what we usually drink. Presumably there is not much of a market for it. Postage stamps cost a bit more. Phone calls to the UK are prohibitively expensive, with no really cheap periods, so the family will have to make do with letters most of the time. But of course it will be many months before we know what the cost of living really is here, for us.

John is snowed under with paperwork for new registration and insurance for the car, but also for a free travel pass for him, being over 65. It will include not just bus and train travel anywhere in the Republic of Ireland but also ferries out (or 'in' as they say here) to many of the islands. Someone told us of a Dublin man with a free over-65's travel pass who went by train to his sister's for lunch every day. She lived in Cork.

May 14 – Tuesday

8.00 am: Every day but one the early morning sun has been clear and bright, lighting up all the white and gold colours in the landscape. I look forward to being able to have breakfast in the Rectory porch that faces south-east, after the walk down the long avenue to the church for Morning Prayer, and back.

5.00 pm: This has been a warm and perfectly sunny day. We had lunch in the cottage garden, and our doors and windows have been open all day. At 2.30 pm I went across to the post office in the hope of sending off some letters, and receiving the incoming mail at the same time. The postman's van arrived and on confirming my name I was given an armful of mail then and there. But Tom, the postman, who bade me welcome and hoped we would all be very happy here, wouldn't take the outgoing mail. He only delivers, he said. The other van would be here in a few minutes.

This evening I am invited to the Mothers' Union meeting in the former school, a few minutes' walk down the road past the Rectory, and tucked into the rocks.

May 15 – Wednesday

The school was closed in 1932, they say. Staring at the varnished wood walls and the broad, brown-painted door of the one-room building, I almost see a ghostly crowd of children. Later, accepting a lift back to the cottage, I learnt that the children I was almost seeing included Nan, and Betty. Probably many of the others I now know too.

I enjoyed the MU meeting last night. Only about a dozen of us, but all nicely informal and democratic – and with a lot of laughter. At the end of the meeting, gone nine o'clock, we have tea and sandwiches and a great many homemade cakes.

This morning I visited some American parishioners whose grandchild, from the Netherlands, I am to baptise on Sunday. It will be Bob's eightieth birthday the same weekend. Friends and family will be flying in from the USA and the Netherlands to help celebrate. What a very varied community this is. Surprised by occasional French, Dutch, German and English voices, I am told that most of them moved her in the 1970s when there was such fear in Europe of nuclear war, and Ireland was the furthest you could go and still be in Europe.

Most of the native Irish population are either farmers or fisherman. Some are retired professional people from the cities. Some are Anglo-Irish. Yet some of the farmers from further along the peninsula have accents so strong I can hardly understand them when they speak. But have been relieved to find that many of the regular Irish people can't always understand them either, unless they can be persuaded to speak more slowly. The accent is intriguing, with an up-and-down lilt that some liken to the Welsh. And some of the pronunciation is different. An 's' is often pronounced 'sh'. 'Th' is sometimes 't' in what I'm told is the Cork City manner, but confusingly others say their 't's as 'th's. I was puzzled by a young woman doing one of the readings in church on Sunday talking about 'Fate'. In the Bible? But no, it was 'faith'. Vowel sounds are not what you might expect. 'Cork' is said as 'Carhk.' You might be 'arhl mahrning in Carhk.' Before we came here we thought we'd try to learn Irish, but perhaps there's no point as almost no-one in these parts speaks it. On the other hand, I was told today, the culture is very definitely Irish.

Nan has promised us a leaflet about the history of the small church next to the Rectory – the 'famine church'. It is the middle of the three churches I am responsible for. It was built almost 150 years ago during the Great Famine, the work providing food or money for the starving local people. Was my predecessor, who organised the scheme, a 'souper' – one of the Anglican clergy who helped the Catholic famine victims but allegedly did it to convert them to Protestantism? It worries me.

On my way into town I saw a heron standing in sea water quite close to the road, not at all bothered by my car.

And today we have been here a week. I still sometimes can't believe we're here at all. What an amazing thing to have done.

May 16 – Thursday – Ascension Day

Six people at the 11.00 am weekday, holy day, service in the town church this morning. Seven people at the 8.00 pm service in the country church. Lovely. They must be making an effort this year because last year there were only two at each. I went to the Community College after the morning service, only to find it closed. This is, after all, Ascension Day, and this is Ireland. (But all the shops were open.)

May 18 – Saturday

The cuckoo was ridiculously noisy this morning, at a little after dawn. Did a set of maybe eighteen or twenty calls at a time, then a slight pause, then started up again. Endlessly, it seemed. I went back to sleep.

Went about thirty miles yesterday evening to the Mothers' Union Diocesan Festival held in a tiny cathedral (the diocese, being a united one, has three). Afterwards, tea and sandwiches and of course tablesful of homemade cakes. I met two people – one clergy, one lay – interested in getting local church people to explore the use of Christian meditation.

John and Rosie and I are occasionally homesick, missing family and friends and the familiar daily life of Norwich. But Rosie is homesick to the point of depression. Not being a driver, she is totally dependent on us to take her about. There are no shops within walking distance. There are buses but only two a day. But she has written a very good misery poem. I hope something good happens for her soon, socially or job-wise or both.

We are fixed up with a local doctor, Larry. Seems lovely. He apologised for not having been at my Institution. He says he can continue to give me the magnesium injections that I'd been having in England ever since I had ME/CFS. I had worried that the Irish health system wouldn't go for it, but I need not have.

May 19 – Sunday

Just back from services in the two main churches: each one a service of Morning Prayer. The one in the town church included the very cosmopolitan baptism, and was a lively and friendly event. It feels all wrong not to be having a Communion service at all on a Sunday. But this pattern of having two Communion services one Sunday and then two Morning Prayer services the next Sunday was set up during the time the parish was without an incumbent, so that a priest needed only to be drafted in once a fortnight: the Morning Prayer services being led by a Lay Reader. Over the next two weeks I'll be changing back to having Holy Communion in one church one week, and Morning Prayer in the other church; and the other way round the following week.

I've rounded up a group of adults and young people to go to a session this evening on help with music and singing for small country churches. It's about an hour's drive away. I guess almost everything is.

It's difficult to find parishioners' houses here as there are usually no full addresses, just the name of the townland, which can be quite a large area with quite a few dwellings in it, but not signposted in any way. People just know where people live. I managed to get hold of a copy of an ancient townlands map of this area, which is better than nothing. And nothing better seems to exist. The only way I will be able to find out where all my parishioners live, and visit them, I'm told, is to be driven around by someone who knows them all, and make a mental (and scribbled) map. Nan has offered.

May 20 – Monday

I thought it was time I began saying Morning Prayer in the church next to the Rectory each day at 8.00 am, as I had been accustomed to do in the parishes where I had previously worked. In the Church of England clergy are required to say Morning and Evening Prayer, at least privately but preferably in church; but not so in the Church of Ireland, I find. When I was interviewed, Nan had mentioned that earlier generations of clergy used to say Morning Prayer in that little church, and they rang the bell to show that they were doing it. She was delighted when I said that I would be doing that.

It is about eight minutes' walk to the church from the cottage where we are temporarily housed, but even in this morning's rain it was a great walk. The early morning sea water in the bay, the smell of the cows which are everywhere, the birdsong, the sight of the first fuchsias in the hedgerows. I shall grow to love that rather dark little church. Ringing the bell, the rope of which is just inside the main door, was not at all as easy as I had imagined. But I expect I will eventually get the hang of it.

The interior of the church is small, and narrow. It seems rather dark because the windows are narrow, and have coloured patterned panes in them. There is a beautiful font, slim and simple, clearly older than the building. At the far end, just before the chancel, there is a small organ on the left, and opposite it the door to the vestry, and the pulpit. The chancel itself is small, and there is only just room to walk between the altar rails and the altar and around the back of the altar. There are three rather splendid stained glass windows showing in the centre the Ascension and on either side a crowd of faces looking upwards.

The music session, in a church in a town I hadn't heard of, was good. Seven of us went, in two cars. The seven included two bright teenagers, Shirley and Caroline, from a devout churchgoing family, and we met with people from other parishes. There was Taizé and unaccompanied singing, and some creative but beautifully simple way of singing the psalms. We agreed that we might be able to do some of this in our own parish. Afterwards there was tea and sandwiches and, of course, lots of homemade cakes.

The outing put my milometer up about a hundred miles. The last sixteen were added by taking the young people home to their remote farmhouse.

The day's post arrives here at 2.30 pm. We have to adjust to this: it feels as if the day hasn't properly begun until the post has arrived. And deliveries are only Monday to Friday anyway. Two days without mail every week is awful. I guess I am a mail addict.

The regional newspapers here take a religious stance as given. 'Farmer expresses devotion to Our Lady,' was the headline over one news story about a man who had built a small shrine on his land. And a tribute in a national paper, by a fairly sophisticated columnist to a deceased journalist colleague included something to the effect that 'he's okay, he's in heaven now.'

This morning I spent nearly three hours with the parish treasurer, learning about parish finance. There is a large bank overdraft, but an overdraft is considered cheaper than owing the diocese money. The treasurer is not worried about the money, only about deceasing parishioners not being replaced by young families because there are fewer and fewer of them in the area. But at least there is the possibility of more retired people moving in, I say.

I learn of the rare Flight & Robson organ, early nineteenth century, in the town church. It has just had £10,000 spent on it. Talented organists, I was told, ought to be invited to give recitals on it, to raise the outstanding £1,200. Now it is thought that the organ in the church by the Rectory is another Flight & Robson, which should be similarly refurbished.

In the afternoon I visited a parishioner in her seventies who was reminiscing about how kitchens (or general living areas) used to be in the old days. 'We had only a pot on a chain when I was a child, and one of those bellows to get the fire going,' she said. Then, as often happened here, she married in her teens a man more than twenty years older, who had been living on his own since his mother died. 'When I came here I didn't know what I'd come into.' Her gestures described primitive domestic chaos. Now her living room is cosy, warm. She enjoys a good talk, she says. We have apple pie and two sorts of cake for tea, just the two of us. I will get very fat here.

She was gently regretting the large numbers of retired foreigners moving into the peninsula. The townland that she grew up in now has only three houses containing families she knew as a child. Then, it supported two football teams of young men.

I feel sad about being English, and thereby increasing the number of 'blow-ins'. I hope we won't speak with noticeably English accents for ever. It isn't just the local accent we'll need to allow to colour our speech, but the

Parts of the Rectory garden

sentence shapes, subtly different, that I suppose we will gradually acquire.

When I get back to the cottage, John and Rosie are listening to a play on the radio. We can only get one television station here. Outside the door the fields are washed in the bright wet evening sunlight.

May 21 – Tuesday

The manager of the small supermarket in town suddenly darted into the shop and whispered 'The funeral's coming now' to one of the assistants and there was a sudden flurry of action. The front doors were closed, all the shop lights were turned off and everyone, staff and customers, stood facing towards the windows. After a few moments the local hearse passed the windows at walking pace, going towards the communal graveyard. Some of the shop staff crossed themselves. The hearse was followed by a few cars and then a crowd of walking people of all ages, including children, and a woman with a small child in a pushchair. It didn't seem particularly solemn: some of the mourners were chatting to each other. Inside the supermarket most of the staff and customers were standing still and quiet. I saw that the fronts of the shops opposite were also darkened and shut.

When the very last of the procession of people, and then cars, had gone by everything opened up again calmly into normal life.

May 22 – Wednesday

'If you visit all your parishioners regularly,' the Bishop had said during my interview with him, 'they will forgive you anything. If you don't visit them regularly they will forgive you nothing.' Yesterday I began the visiting in earnest. With Nan in the passenger seat I drove down winding roads, up craggy lanes, into muddy yards and off again around the sides of the hills. And everywhere we stopped to say hello to people. Whether I will be able next time to find all these places and all these people on my own is another thing altogether. But we had a wonderful morning – no, more than a morning.

Maybe I can't call it a local characteristic on the basis of two people, but the two I have spent a working morning with, Jenny and Nan, don't seem to notice lunch time at all. 'Are you alright for one more visit?' Nan asked at 3.00 pm. We'd started out at 11.00 am. I knew John would be waiting for the car by now so we couldn't do that one more visit. Of course I wasn't hungry because we'd been given coffee and cake at every stop, and at one English home a large sherry. We were trying not to stop too long anywhere, just to have a quick look-in so that I could be introduced to any parishioners I had not yet met, and make my mental and scribbled map of where they lived. But sometimes there were pastoral reasons why it was better not to be too brief: and I was impressed by how sensitive Nan was to this. She is great. Small, wiry, dignified, very bright and rather stern; but amazingly charitable, non-judgmental. We found out the other day that she is in her eighties. Hard to believe.

The visits we made were a microcosm of the parishioners here. An Irishman with a very English accent who had spent many years in Africa. A very English woman in a tiny cottage that was all traditional

Irish on the outside and all modern sliding glass doors on the inside. A woman of indeterminable age but described in advance as 'like a child,' in a farm kitchen dark and ancient, her carer sister temporarily absent. And a whole range of women of all ages in their sitting rooms and kitchens while their menfolk were at work, mostly on the farm; but one was away in their small garlic-butter factory and one, retired, was out playing golf. I met fourteen parishioners in all this day.

Today I sorted the registers and parish records for all four churches, including the one that was closed down by the diocese in 1991, just five years ago, causing a great deal of grief and not a little anger. Some registers are missing. There is nothing prior to the 1960s in some cases. But Nan tells me that is partly because many of the really old ones were stored in the Public Records Office in Dublin and were destroyed in a fire there in the civil war in 1922. But also because of the famous Revd B. that everyone tells me about. A former curate in the parish, it seems that he insists he is still the true incumbent. When he was displaced he took some of the registers and some of the church silver as hostages. Now in his nineties he lives just a few miles from here. The Archdeacon is still in touch with him on reasonably amicable terms and still hoping for the return of plate and books.

Nan has now given us some papers about one of my predecessors, the Revd William Fisher, who had the country church built in the days of the great famine here. John and Rosie have become very interested and are typing out what we hope will be a leaflet about him for sale in the church next year. Because next year, it seems, is the 150th anniversary of the building of the church. The parish will have to do something fairly spectacular.

May 24 – Friday

It was still dark when I woke to a phone call from D. Could I come, he asked, because his mother was after dying. I had visited them but didn't know her health was in question. I drove through the twisty lanes, still unfamiliar and confusing in the dark. Several other people, neighbours, were already in the cottage. Almost straight away we all went up the narrow stairs, squeezing around the narrow bed in the narrow room. Mother laid peacefully, her arms having been crossed on her chest, and a scarf placed under her chin and tied on top of her head. 'So her jaw doesn't drop,' D. said. I took out my book of prayers. Most of those present would be Catholic. There was a calm reverence in the room, and we joined together in the Lord's Prayer, the 'Our Father'.

Then we went down to the kitchen. The whiskey was poured in a miscellany of cups and glasses, and the gentle chat began, and D. was condoled with touches and kind words. Eventually the doctor arrived and the rest of us dispersed into the dawn.

May 25 – Saturday

Yesterday John and I went into town to see variously the gardaí for some necessary paperwork, the doctor for my injection, and the coalman for a sack of coal. All three had said they would be there at specific times. In the event none of them was. But of course the doctor and the garda are both single-handed. And I did get my injection, from the district nurse who had been at my institution.

After that I went visiting in and near the town. But only managed one out of town visit in the remainder of the morning, at a farm on the bay. A lovely couple, but what with coffee and cakes, and being shown a video of their daughter's wedding, it took about an hour and a half. People here, I find, don't want to put the kettle on until you've been there about three-quarters of an hour. And I can't really see how to speed that bit up.

I did two visits in the afternoon, in the town centre. From all three visits I learnt a great deal about my immediate predecessor and about parish politics in general. And – implicitly or explicitly – about people's expectations that I will draw the parish together again, and bring back those who left it for one reason or

The town centre

another. 'We hear they are expecting miracles,' one non-churchgoing summer resident said to John and me when we went to supper with them last night.

We have been told about road bowling. A County Cork speciality – though a few other counties also do it – it takes place on various local roads here, but mostly the one that winds north out of the town. Two players take it in turn to hurl a small very heavy iron ball (called a 'bowl,' rhyming with 'owl') with great force and accuracy along the twisting road, to see which of them can get to the end of the course in the least number of throws. The course is over two miles long. The road is not closed, but cars and other vehicles must stop and wait until they can be beckoned through. What I forgot to ask was when his happens. I expect we will find out.

10.00 am. Sunny. I am writing a sermon with the cottage door open, daisies thick on the grass, birds chirping. We are going for a meal this evening to the restaurant just down the road. Run by a family who are signed-up parishioners but non-churchgoers.

May 26 – Sunday

Two more lovely services today. Although both the churches are very good at providing people to read the lessons, one church is much better than the other at providing volunteers to lead the prayers, the setting up of the altar, and looking after the linens, etc. It's odd how that sort of thing goes by the place, often for years and years despite the turnover of people – and, in this case, both places having the same incumbent.

People here are wonderfully ready to comment on the sermon. Even the ex-patriate or summer resident English seem more relaxed than in England, and say things like 'After that' (my Ascension sermon) 'I look forward to your Trinity Sunday sermon.' Irish parishioners, though, are more likely to say that a sermon has been helpful or thought-provoking. Nan, to whom I had apologised for the fact that as organist she had had to hear the same sermon at both churches that day, said very movingly, 'No; they are food and drink to me.'

I was cheered to see a member of what I had yesterday called the non-churchgoing restaurant family in church this morning.

Today the wind got up as I was driving from the town church to the country church. And inside the narrow building it is like a gale. People say this has been the worst May for many years – but that's true of Britain as well, apparently. I'm glad that we had those beautiful days when we first arrived at the beginning of the month, to show us that it *can* be like here. Now, looking out of the cottage window, I can see a very light rain being driven horizontally from the west. John says someone told him the other day that what they have here is 'the *soft* rain – but it's quite wet.'

Later: We went for a Sunday afternoon drive, like tourists. We wanted to drive the long zagged road up onto Mount G., even though its peak was hidden in rain mist. Lying unobtrusively behind the town, this is the only elevation in the parish grand enough to be called a mountain. Not technically, however: it is just over 1,300 feet. A driveable track wound steeply up with an unnerving drop on one side. But we came to a closed gate, and found that the last stretch has to be done on foot. Perhaps on a better day we will.

We came back around the coast road, and stopped at the dolmen that is between the road and the sea, just a few hundred yards from the Rectory gateway. Its opening faces across the bay towards where, in red glory or grey rain, the sun will set. There is an information board here (such communication is rare in this country, where even the local hospital is unidentified by any sort of name-board). It says it is a Bronze Age wedge tomb, built around 3000-2000 BCE. Ancient religious use of the stones ceased in Christian times, but was briefly resumed in the eighteenth century when priests were forbidden to say Mass in churches. You can stand by the monument with its ghosts of prehistoric and more recent worshippers

The dolmen near the Rectory gateway

and be thumped and knocked about by the wind and almost deafened by the sound of the Atlantic breaking on the nearby rocks and stones, and the centuries become mere days.

In a few minutes we are going to the town for an evening of 'box, fiddle and guitar' music and sett dancing, not in our usual small crowded noisy two-room bar, but in the bar and rooms behind one of the food shops.

May 27 – Monday

The gorse is fading now, and the wild garlic is finally beginning to droop. But suddenly there are masses of sea-pinks and dog daisies. Bees are all over the purple vetch, and the fuchsia is everywhere in bud in the hedges. This morning on the way back from Morning Prayer in the little church I picked some fiddle-heads of bracken to cook and eat. When we are finally moved into the Rectory I shall miss this half-mile walk from the cottage to the church, with the horizon of rocks and hills changing subtly in light and shape as I follow the road that curves around the bay.

The builders have finished at the Rectory and an army of parishioners, middle-aged and older, have moved in to begin the painting. John and Rosie have joined them. 'Two weeks,' churchwarden Billy says, 'you'll be in here in two weeks.' John is painting the raw shelves in my study, and says I will be able to put books on them in a day or two. That will feel like a real advance.

We had a good evening yesterday. There was, unusually, an entrance fee for the music and dancing, and we learnt that it was in aid of the town's attempt to buy a yawl. There is much sailing interest and activity in the town, but they have not in recent years been able to enter the annual southwest coast yawl race, although they have acquired an old boat. Fundraising for a new one began eight weeks ago, and one man I spoke to there – a parishioner – spoke confidently of raising the necessary £10,000 in time for next year's race. 'We raised seventy-five thousand for the planetarium,' he said, 'just because a German offered us his spare set of optical lenses.' The planetarium, in the grounds of the Community College, is now one of the town's main attractions.

We got to know more people last night. A pleasant, good-looking young fisherman in yellow boots came in, and looked intently in our direction. Working his way through the crowd he got through and began a lively conversation with John and me. We squeezed up and made room for him to sit. But his eyes were on Rosie. And gradually his conversation was being called across to Rosie. I suggested we changed places so they could sit next to each other. Rosie was embarrassed but clearly pleased. The rest of the evening was theirs, and by the end of it they had a date for next Saturday.

Nan has lent us another batch of papers about the Revd Mr Fisher, this time the script of a television play about him by Eoghan Harris. The play was produced by the Irish broadcasting company, RTÉ, in conjunction with BBC2 but was never shown by either. 'Controversial,' according to a newspaper story about its filming. This copy of the script is inscribed by Harris to Nan 'with affection': she was helpful to him when he came to the area. But the rector of that time declined to allow the church to be used in the filming, saying something to the effect that it would stir up old Catholic-Protestant wounds. Which was probably true. The whole subject becomes more and more gripping. As is the whole history of the last few centuries here. I am fascinated by the existence among my parishioners of so many Huguenot names. Am I imagining it, or do I really see very Huguenot faces? They did apparently flee to Ireland in the late seventeenth and early eighteenth centuries from southern France where they had been persecuted. When we were staying in France a few years ago, in the Cevennes, the history of those people was all around us. I remember most vividly the Huguenot Musée du Desert, but also the church service of their descendants in the town of Anduze, and the open air service among twisted trees on acres of uneven land. And here are the French names, many anglicised out of recognition until you say them aloud.

Today I have done more visiting. Now I have met sixteen more families or individuals. Ninety-three more to do. And that's just for first visits.

In the farming community it is always into the kitchen that I am invited. There are usually several upright chairs, placed with their backs against the walls, and no matter how big the room or how many people are in it, everyone sits on those chairs, upright, knees together, hands loosely linked. This manner of socialising must surely have come down from the eighteenth century. We talk, looking from face to face, and it is like watching a tennis match.

Driving about the parish would be a lot easier if a detailed map was available, but so far there is not one. The newsagent says one is to be published soon. Meanwhile I manage partly with a half-inch to the mile Ordnance Survey map, to get an overall view. But I also need the more detailed townland maps I've been given, because the OS map gives hardly any townlands. Yet people's addresses are simply their townland. When we went for supper with some summer residents they showed us some wonderful old maps, very large but showing every field. They said they'd paid about £35 for each of them.

Then the other day, when I was sorting out old papers and books left in the Rectory study by the previous incumbent I found a cardboard tube with some rolled papers inside, and out came two maps of that very same sort, 1901 and 1902, six inches to the mile, covering most of the parish. What a joy! I have a passion for maps, but to find these when they were just what I need is pure pleasure. (Oddly, there were a shop's modern price stickers on them: they had been bought fairly recently at £2.75 each.) The only difference from those expensive ones is that those were coloured.)

May 28 – Tuesday

Today we all went into the big town of Bantry, half an hour's drive, for me to visit a parishioner in hospital there – having phoned yesterday to ascertain that he was still there – and for Rosie to have a 10.00 am interview with Social Services as she is currently unemployed. She was nervous about it, rehearsing in the car possible answers to possibly difficult questions, and remembering long dole queues and tough interviewers in Norwich. It was all over in five minutes. She was the only one in the office when it opened. They knew who she was before she identified herself, merely asked if she would be looking for work, and whether meanwhile she had any income; and told her how to get an interim payment if she needed it.

I found the hospital, thanks to some beaming nuns, and walked down bright corridors with large statues of the Virgin or particular saints at every turning. I found the ward but was told Mr R. had gone home yesterday. 'You must be the new lady Rector,' one of the staff said chattily as we walked back down the corridor together. 'Are you in the Rectory yet, or are they still working on it?' This was the town of a neighbouring large parish, nearly twenty miles from our Rectory. How could she possibly know about us? But I didn't query it. I begin to take such grapevine efficiency for granted.

The other day when I went for the first time into the bank in our own little town, the bank manager (who had been at my institution) leaned over the counter to greet me warmly, and to chat about the Rectory, and life in general, while other customers waited with no sign of impatience. I expect they were interested in the conversation anyway.

Looking for an Irish dictionary in the bookshop in our town we found that a great deal has been published about different aspects of the great famine. We also discovered that Eoghan Harris's television play re-emerged as a stage play at the Abbey Theatre in Dublin. Its title, 'Souper Sullivan,' was suddenly familiar and I remembered reading about it in the English papers at some time. The controversy centres on souperism (*see May*

15). An essay in one of the books we browsed, but failed then to buy, suggested that the issue is very complex. But so interesting. We should have bought the book. We will have to get to a bigger library than the cosy one in our small town and do some serious reading on it all.

May 29 – Wednesday

John need not have worried that all my parishioners would be dour Protestant teetotallers. In my visiting today a retired bank manager urged me to have a large glass of sherry with my 4.00 pm tea and cake. And earlier, by a farming couple in an old-fashioned farmhouse, to have a very large whiskey with my 11.00 am tea and cakes. It felt impolite to ask for a smaller glass to decant some into, but I did still have a good bit of driving to do. The farmhouse is not the *House and Gardens* type of old-fashioned, but is truly old-fashioned: all cream paint and American cloth and lino, and functioning cannisters and boxes and tins ranged neatly along the thin high shelf above the dark cream range. We talk about cows, and the wife speaks very interestingly about their love of music.

So many of these old houses take me right back to times of my childhood spent in rural Wales: not just visually but often by the smell of them. Neither good nor bad, just different – and lost to me until now. How have they managed not to change when all the rest of the world has? But that seems true of so much of what we've experienced of this lovely country. – I try to identify the smells and can't, without seeming rudely abstracted.

That reminds me of David Thomson's book *Wood-brook*, given to us by friends just before we left England. A very evocative account of an Irish estate, the landlords and the country people, just before the Second World War. In it, he says somewhere that in thinking of the past it is smells that he remembers most. That seems odd: I can't remember a smell by wanting to. But suddenly catching a smell that stuns you by re-presenting another time and place – that is powerful. These past weeks, perhaps because of the sensitivity to odours that goes with being in a new place, I have had re-presented to me childhood times not only in Wales and in north London, but even in the vegetation of Canada, and of Massachusetts. Just fleetingly, just long enough to identify it, then it's gone.

The painting of the Rectory is going amazingly fast. We might be in there in a week. What a wonderful thought. We are getting increasingly restless, partly because so many of the things we need – clothes, and kitchenware, and for me especially my theological and liturgical and pastoral books and papers – are unlocatable in the piled-up boxes we packed so many weeks ago. And partly because we know there will be so much to do, when we finally get into the house, to make it a home.

The heron that I saw once by the road I have seen again in the same place, this time flying overhead and landing. But there is a heron (another one? the same one? I know nothing about birds) that I have seen several times now in our bay when the tide is out. The smell of the seaweed when the tide is out is blissful. And today I have seen – how long has it been there? – a great bed of wild yellow irises on the wet ground between the bay and the road wall.

May 30 – Thursday

Visited an elderly couple just down the road yesterday evening. She turned out to be the sister of the woman I visited that morning, several miles away. I was warned when I first came here that everyone is related to everyone else. In the farming community, that is. They are kindly about my efforts at bell-ringing in the mornings. He used to do it on Sundays. I will be able to do it properly in a few months, he thinks. Pathetic, really – it's not as if it's real bell-ringing. There is only the one.

Workhouse ruins

This morning I started visiting early, in order to catch the farmer I had failed to see the other day in Bantry hospital because he had gone home. Nan was worried about that, because years ago after a hernia operation he went out lifting bales the next day, and burst his stitches. I had tried to see him yesterday but the neat farmyard was bare, tractor-less and dog-less; there were only some hens wandering softly around. I went that time to his neighbour, who hadn't seen him and was worried, since the tractor was gone, that he'd gone back to work so soon. But this morning I found him at home. A big man, elderly, with a large sweet face. I got a beautiful smile, and words of welcome. His bachelor kitchen was wonderfully clean and tidy. Again, lino and American cloth, cannisters on the high shelf, but here the upper half of the wall was painted sunshine yellow, and the lower half – including a long wooden seat with a high curved back – bright blue.

They need not have worried about him. He is waiting for an appointment for an angiogram at the hospital in Cork and is dutifully resting. He had been lying down on the long seat until he heard my car come into the yard. On the other hand, the reason he had been out yesterday when I called was because his old car had died under him, and he had gone into town on the tractor to buy another less elderly car. Didn't need a new one: he didn't drive very often as it wasn't good for his heart. I didn't say that driving a tractor into town was probably even less good for it. But I did ask who was looking after the farm work. He has good neighbours, he said, so that he only has to 'keep the place tidy.' Did he want me to bring him Holy Communion, I enquired, as local clergy had been doing while he was in hospital, but he said he was planning on coming to church on Sunday, with one of the neighbours. When I left it was with a present of some eggs, and more kind welcoming words.

Leaving the farm I met a herd of cows coming up the narrow lane from the farm below, and eventually there emerged from behind them a young lad, and then two more: three farming brothers who live in a tiny cottage. One of them is still at school; the other two are not much older. This young one when he passed me was so shy that he didn't look at me and could barely return my greeting. I wondered what sort of life they will lead as they grow older. I had thought that the old Irish pattern of shy farmers not marrying until they were middle-aged was something from the past. Now I'm not so sure.

The ink cartridge of my computer printer ran out last night. I have a spare one somewhere among the mountain of boxes in the Rectory, but there's no way I can get at it. John asks the computer people in town but they don't stock them. They suggest a few places that might, and could perhaps deliver it to them for us to pick up. I phone one of those places in a town forty or fifty miles away. Could they phone me back, they say, because they will have to phone Dublin for one. To think that I just used to wander into a shop in Norwich and buy one!

The weather has been fierce in the later part of the day, with billowing rain, and in the outer bay the waves are hurling themselves in huge white throws against the rocks. More rain forecast for the next few days. 'Worst May in forty years,' people are saying. We mustn't take it personally.

June 1 – Saturday

A message this morning to say that a dear friend in Norwich has died. This is when the distance is bad. Talking on the phone to people is not the same as being there with them at a time like this.

Last night, after a very pleasant bit of bar-socialising and music in the town, we found ourselves driving back into a dramatic landscape. It must have been about eleven o'clock, yet there was still some light in the sky above the hills, so that the horizon was blue-grey, cream, and dark grey. I pulled off the road near the dolmen to get a better look at the sea. We watched the waves bashing, smashing onto the rocks, with a nearly full moon behind them. This is real sea and an exhilaratingly wild landscape. Rosie stood on the cliffs like the French Lieutenant's Woman. John said this was like something you see on television and assume you will never see it for real; yet here we are.

June 3 – Monday

It's probably because I've got some sort of mild 'flu (that kindly waited until the Sunday services were over to manifest itself yesterday evening) that I am feeling very jaundiced about Ireland at the moment. Irritated at how difficult it is to get the simplest things and how expensive everything is. Mostly this last, especially as we can't see why it should be. Taxes, both direct and indirect, are horrific here and yet what are they for, what are they spent on? If there were a great public health service, and wonderful public transport and huge government subsidies for the arts and sport, it would be acceptable.

The education system seems very good, though I'm not sure that's due to money. But other public services are lamentable or very basic. People here cynically say the money all goes on the government itself. It's hard to see what else can account for the state of things.

And the Church of Ireland seems to have a similar problem. People in the parishes complain, as people in parishes always do, about the money that goes up to 'them' – the diocesan and national coffers. But here they may have a different and legitimate case. For example, the General Synod of the Church of Ireland – its governing body in effect – has over 600 members. That's about a hundred more than the General Synod of the very much larger Church of England. Norwich Diocese, with 220 active clergy, has five clergy members on Synod, including the bishop and an archdeacon. And five lay members. The Irish diocese I am in now has twenty-five active clergy, of whom fourteen are members of Synod. And there are twenty-eight lay members. If accommodation and meals have to be paid for all these people to attend national Synod meetings the burden of such expense falling on a relatively small church must be heavy. But perhaps they all pay their own expenses?

While I'm complaining I may as well go on to say how depressing the media is here. We can only get RTÉ 1 on the television that is in the cottage and it is, on the whole, appalling. If it were a public service station it wouldn't be so bad, but it is a commercial station so we have mainly amateurish commercials *and* lousy programming. Newspapers and magazines are embarrassingly poorly written and presented. Why should all this be so in a country that is flowing with verbal and literary talent?

Perhaps I'd hate it – yes, I would – if Ireland suddenly burst out into gaudy hoardings and billboards and neon lights and bombardments of commercial information. The absence of those is a pleasure. But something hallway between that and the total lack of such information would be good. Forthcoming local events are generally only advertised by word of mouth. Finding a 'religious goods' supplier in the diocesan directory was just about impossible. It has over 500 ads, spread through the pages. There is an index, but it is not organised by the type of services offered. It is just the names of the businesses arranged in a sort of alphabetical order – but randomly within each letter of the alphabet. Each has then only a one or two word description, like 'butcher' or – in the case of the one from which I hoped to purchase communion wafers – 'clothing'! In the end I used the yellow pages of the phone book.

Having 'flu can also make you very homesick.

Later: From midday onwards I've felt human again. Optimistic, and interested in things, and glad to be here. What a relief.

Rosie had a good evening with her new beau on Saturday. His name is Richie.

We have been lent more material about the controversial Revd William Fisher, but also incidentally about life in this part of the country over the past hundred years or so. Fascinating stuff. Plenty of material for a couple of leaflets for tourists and other visitors.

June 4 – Tuesday

I've found out that the triple stained glass window in the little church where I say Morning Prayer was made by Joshua Clarke & Sons of Dublin. Clarke? And yes, the name is not a coincidence. The artist Harry Clarke, who has done such amazing stained glass work in so many places, was Joshua's son. He worked with him from 1914 onwards and then took over the firm in 1921. This window was put in place in 1909. But just possibly Harry C. had a hand in it …

June 5 – Wednesday

I have had to relearn how to drive. I've always known you are supposed to have your hands at the 'ten-to-two' position on the steering wheel, but have lazily preferred twenty-to-four. Now I have to do it properly because everyone driving here salutes everyone they know with an odd little right-hand index-finger gesture, made without removing the hand from the wheel. It requires enormous alertness to identify the car and the driver in time to do it, especially on windey lanes, and I fail again and again, being frequently saluted by people I have not recognised. Perhaps the safest thing is to salute everyone with a registration plate of this county. If they don't know me it won't matter, and if they do I won't have snubbed them.

Planning permission here is not as advanced (or nanny-ish?) as in England. People are still allowed to have those wonderful small first storey windows that, inside the house, are almost at ankle level, with the eaves coming down to about waist level. So many English vernacular houses have been ruined by pushing dormer windows up above the roof level.

Some interesting things from the newspapers we have been reading: firstly, the name of this townland, which someone told us meant 'hill by the river' is thought by others to mean 'great tower'. But there is no trace of one. Although it is written on all the maps, even the 1902 one, as beginning with a 'T', many of the older people pronounce it as 'Th'. And that's the proper spelling of the 'tower' part of the word. Memory is obviously very long here.

Secondly, until recently the word 'afternoon' was not used here. As it says in the Book of Genesis, there was morning and there was evening. When one of the parishioners had agreed on an evening meeting, and I went on to ask her what time it should be, she suggested four o'clock. It had vaguely puzzled me at the time.

There is said to be a ghost in one of the rocky fields that we haven't yet been able to get to, behind the Rectory. A golden haired woman. And – somewhere back up there – the Revd Mr Fisher had a vegetable garden. It *isn't* just a myth.

The army of painters at the Rectory has finished. Today the woodworm spraying is being done. The carpets are to be laid this weekend in the three reception rooms and on the stairs. Tiles for the bathroom have been ordered and will be put in early next week. Then we can move in. How good that will be.

A swarm of bees appeared a few days ago, high up on the gutter of the Rectory roof. We had seen or heard a request to be called if any swarms were found, but couldn't remember where we'd seen or heard it. A day later there was a sort of travelling hive on the back lawn, and the next day some of the bees were crawling about in it. Someone had obviously called someone. Nobody is very sure who it is, but it is nice that someone is doing it.

In these early June evenings there is still some light in the sky at 11.00 pm. I suppose we are so much further west here, but on the same time band as Norwich. I heard a cuckoo still going at something past ten o'clock the other night. Silver light on a late afternoon makes the bay at low tide look like a John Sell Cotman painting of his 1804 – 1810 style: flat areas of over-simplified colour-washes, like a heavenly painting by numbers.

June 7 – Friday

The ink cartridge for my computer printer finally arrived on Wednesday – only it wasn't. It was for a totally different machine. I fumed with frustration. And decided I would have to go to Cork and try to get one. So I took yesterday as my day off and we set out, all three of us, for urban delights.

It took us over two hours to get there, going through three towns as there are virtually no bypasses. But the towns were interesting, each one different and seeming to have its own personality.

Cork, we were relieved to find, is a pleasant city, fairly small, and friendly, relaxed and wide-streeted, and with a good library and interesting places to eat. We spent the whole day there. I did get an ink cartridge – the right one – though admittedly at a price fifty per cent higher than in England. Then we found a shop selling surprisingly low-priced curtain fabric, and impulsively bought what was needed for the dining room and my study. The parish is to reimburse us for these. Then, stirred into financial rashness, we found a nearby hardware store and arranged to buy the lawn mower we so definitely need, and a wheelbarrow too. Only, we knew we couldn't fit them into the car with the three of us, and they didn't deliver so far away, so elaborate arrangements have been made for me to pick them up on Sunday evening before I go to an ordination service at the cathedral. This involved having a very long and friendly chat with the two male shop assistants, about my job, and the Rectory, which they knew and people they had known in our area (all this sixty or seventy miles away). Transactions in shops – even in the city, apparently – take a long time because of the chats. Buying the ink cartridge had involved a lengthy discussion about archaeology, though I can't remember how we got onto that.

A two-hour drive back to Nan's cottage. Tired but – yes – happy.

June 8 – Saturday

The exterior of the Rectory has been cleaned and then sprayed under pressure, in preparation for painting, and already it looks so much better that it will soon be hard to remember its former greyness. It's going to be a *lovely* house. Suddenly I realise we have been here a month today.

Summer 1996

June 11 – Tuesday

There was an ordination service in Cork Cathedral on Sunday. I had hoped it would be a great event and I would meet a lot of the diocesan clergy there. But it was disappointing: of those who were there, most seemed to be retired.

I should have gone to the tea-and-cakes afterwards but was so depressed by the service that instead I headed back for the car and the long drive home. The whole thing had appeared to be unrehearsed, with people not knowing what they were meant to be doing, or when. It was late in beginning: we robed clergy just stood around 'backstage' in a bored silence for a long, long time. The liturgical content was dull, and the choral singing ragged and slow: quite dreadful. Naturally, I don't want services of worship to be run like military operations, but only when everything runs smoothly and is of the best standard reachable, can we all be free to engage fully in worship. Much of the language of the service was exclusive, in gender terms, and I thought wearily that all that work would have to be gone through again: though I was encouraged by talking with Olive, a very lively and young clergywoman who was at least as irritated by the language as I was. Talking with her was for me the best part of that day.

Today's post included the communion wafers I had ordered from a convent in Cork. Almost all the Church of Ireland parishes here, it seems, use ordinary bread in their Communion services. I know that in some places that is seen as a good modern thing to do, but there are practical problems such as the amount of crumbs it makes. Then last week I discovered that one of my parishioners is on a gluten-free diet for medical reasons and therefore felt she could not receive Holy Communion with everyone else. I said that was awful, and promised to find gluten-free wafers. Having to order those I thought I might as well order a batch of traditional wafers as well. I put a note about it in the new weekly parish newssheet ('What sort of bread did Jesus use?') and said that I would be using wafers as well as bread. No cries of outrage have reached my ears yet. So far. And a neighbouring incumbent, somewhat more 'high church' than the average Irish clergyperson, did tell me that wafers were not unknown in the Church of Ireland.

Yesterday I met with Father Hurley, the 'Parish Priest'. That means he is the Catholic priest of the area, not the Anglican one, like me. In fact the Church of Ireland does not really use the word 'priest' of its clergy. Which is,

I suppose, part of the wish to keep a clearly defined distinction between 'them' and 'us'. How sad it is.

Father Hurley is one of the two Catholic priests of this peninsula. I liked him very much. There was some sense of a barrier, which at first disappointed me, as so many had told me how ecumenically minded he was. In Norwich we Anglican clergy had been accustomed to having a very relaxed relationship with the priest of the Catholic Cathedral. Then I reminded myself that very few Catholic priests in Ireland are accustomed to working with women ministers of any denomination.

Next week we will have the first of our parish's Select Vestry meeting to be held since my arrival. This is the equivalent of a Parochial Church Council (PCC) meeting in England. I asked one of the Vestry officers about an agenda: who draws it up, is it presented on paper at the meeting or in advance of it? 'Oh, we don't have an agenda,' was the answer. 'That way you as Rector can put on what you like, or leave it off at the last minute if that seems better.' I feel I *ought* to appreciate the relaxed Irishness of that.

I have started producing a monthly parish newsletter – just a one-sheet, folded paper with a photo or drawing on the front. A good way not only of providing information about services and events, but also miscellaneous information that keeps people in touch.

John has been eyeing the one and only fish-and-chip shop in the area, always hoping to find it open, or at least to see a notice of its opening hours. The reason there is no list, we found out, is that the shop's opening depends on

A fine West Cork sky

whether there is any fish – and whether the proprietor is in the mood to open.

People are so patient here. As drivers they wait patiently for each other to negotiate the randomly parked cars in the town, and the lumpy road surfaces, as if none of them was ever in a hurry. Yesterday in the town a young boy on a bike coming the opposite way stopped his ride and gestured that I could turn right, in front of him, and would not accept my gesture of asking him to proceed before I turned.

Today we have been at the Rectory, moving boxes and furniture around so that Billy can do the last of the anti-wood-worming. The phone kept ringing, and twice I had to lead parishioners into my desk-less and chair-less study for various consultations. Not having been on the phone has been a serious handicap: being on it is going to be quite energetic.

When we got back to the cottage we thought at first there was no post. We had not left the door or windows open for the postman, as we do if we are just going out for an hour or two. And the message that he should leave the post with Nan at the post office had obviously not got through to him. 'We'll have to wait now, until tomorrow,' we thought. A while later, John went upstairs and found the post – including a small package – inside the bedroom window. Postman Tom, determined and resourceful, must have stood on the downstairs windowsill and pushed the post up into the open top half of the upstairs window.

June 12 – Wednesday

At last I can ring the church bell properly: this morning I managed to ring three sets of three rings. Which of course is how the Angelus is rung from the Catholic church in town. I hope no one is going to object. Or even worse, object but not tell me.

June 15 – Friday

No time to write this now – yesterday we moved into the Rectory. I say 'we' but it was mostly John and Rosie who did the work, as I had a fairly normal schedule of visiting to fill, and today a sermon (and a service sheet) to write. However, we worked so hard that we had fish and chips (yes!) for supper; and it was achingly difficult to get up when the alarm went off this morning.

Those English friends who said the weather never gets hot in Ireland could be wrong. It has turned quite startlingly warm.

June 18 – Tuesday

The unpacking is finally all done, but every spare moment is obsessively filled with moving things from where they randomly are to where we want them to be. So much of this would have been done by the removal men if we'd had just a one-stage removal. My four filing cabinets are still out in the porch.

The days are beautifully sunny and warm. Last night we were driving home from an unexpected invitation from a total stranger to 'drinks at 6.00 pm', a small gathering so envigoratingly mixed-European that we didn't leave until 9.00 pm; and the mountain and the rocky slopes looked different yet again in this new climate. The hills seemed ranged one behind the other, misty yet distinctly outlined, like a Japanese painting, and all a soft grey-pink. When the road reached the bay we saw the sea water flat and silver, like polished steel among the soft pink rocks and the dark sky. We were stunned, said things, but our words are too small for such glory.

Checking my parish visiting list today I find I have visited – or in other ways spent time with – nearly fifty of the 113 households on the list.

On Sunday evening (that is, at 4.00 pm) the Parish Priest and I blessed the town's newly acquired yawl, the *Fastnet Flyer 1*, at a ceremony on the pier attended by several hundred people. This is a second-hand yawl, clinker built: the fundraising goes on to obtain a new and faster fibreglass boat, but £5,000 is already in. After the blessing and prayer and the champagne popping and balloon releasing, three of the famed W. brothers

*Hilary and the local Parish Priest helping to launch
the yawl, Fastnet Flyer 1*

('rowing since they were babies'), with one other rower, and a young lad as cox, leapt in and rowed the boat for the first time in public, around the pier and out into the harbour, away out of sight.

A group of young Canadians are staying for a few weeks at the backpackers' hostel in the town. They are in Ireland to take part in an international marine event, the Atlantic Challenge. One of them came to church, and afterwards asked if he could play the organ. Both our regular organists are away next week so the young man has agreed to play. His name is William; he is a nomadic Inuit, and until last Friday was hunting caribou. The readings at the country church were read on Sunday by Lilian, a black woman from Zimbabwe who is living here now. And all this in a remote corner of Ireland.

More launch festivities

June 19 – Wednesday

'It will be the summer coming now, surely,' our neighbour Hilda says, stopping in the lane to talk to me. Most people are hoping for a repeat of last year's four months of warm weather. Meanwhile the roadsides bristle with fuchsia, and fox gloves and dog daisies crowd the green banks, the fields are awash with buttercups, and the sea-air-loving escallonia splashes the hedges with deep pink. There is a spindly cerise-coloured flower here and there which is quite unfamiliar until we look closely: it resembles a primitive gladiolus.

John and I were initiated a few days ago into the playing of croquet. Our hosts were Irish but quite a few of the other twelve players were English 'blow-ins'.

The game was followed, of course, by a gracious tea of sandwiches and cakes. An interesting experience. But I don't think I'm the right person for it. It takes hours for everyone to play, which is fine if you aren't longing or needing to do lots of other things as well.

Our post today included several letters from family and friends. Wonderful. Rosie has been offered a job by the restaurant where we went for dinner when we were new here, and is saying she will need new clothes. I suggest waiting until she knows she likes the work. Thoreau had something when he said: 'Beware of enterprises that call for new clothes.'

June 20 – Thursday

I have been told a sad life story today – and have actually heard very little of it. Lizzie, whom I went to visit in a psychiatric hospital miles outside the parish, is gentle and sweet, and intelligent. She chatted, cried, smiled, theologised; and asked with interest about me and my family. I could understand her easily, even though she comes from the farms – I say that because with some of the far west farmers I find difficult to understand their words. But sometimes her voice sank so low that even though she leaned her head against mine I couldn't make out the details of what she was telling me about something that had happened. Later, I told Betty I had seen her, because I know she visits her. Betty said the very thing that I had been wondering about: that she would like to take her out for the day. 'But I think she wouldn't want to go back in.' Anyway, I had told Lizzie that I would see her again soon.

June 21 – Friday

Bread is real food here. Very little of the wrapped-sliced
sort is on sale: even in the supermarkets most of the
white bread is what is now called in England 'bakers'
bread' – but here it is closer to homemade bread than
even the best of the bread we could get in Norwich. Or
there is soda bread, brown with or without cornmeal
in, or white and with currants. Buttermilk, which I used
to pay the earth for in England when I wanted to make
soda bread or scones, is about the same price as ordinary
milk here. It has a fairly long life and a batch of fresh
soda bread can be mixed and set in the oven at home in
a few minutes. Apple pies, also looking homemade, are
found everywhere from Nan's Post Office shop to the big
town supermarkets. They have a lovely soft and rather
cake-y pastry – I'm told Irish bakers put an egg in pie
pastry. Our local supermarket has about the best tiny
profiteroles I have ever eaten, with whipped cream and
good chocolate icing, for 15p each.

This really is a foreign country. Last night I
experienced my first Select Vestry meeting. I knew
already that its members did not expect to have an
agenda of any sort. I am beginning to know that they do
not expect any sort of forward planning, either. When I
asked about dates for future events such as the Harvest
Thanksgiving, or next year's Garden Party – for which a
large amount of preparation is needed – there was a sort
of puzzled lack of interest. A woman in her forties, who
came from England twenty-odd years ago, interpreted
for me. 'We're not usually that organised,' she said.

Decision making is difficult too. I got agreement about using wafers rather than sliced white bread for Holy Communion. But on other matters, such as second or larger notice boards outside the churches, for changeable notices such as special services, cake sales or Mothers' Union events, I couldn't get a Yes *or* a No. (Like the Norfolk village council John remembers, where two men present didn't vote Aye or No – and then declined to abstain.)

The people here are keen to have parish events, but don't worry in advance about planning them. I am told that they just happen: people will do things when the time comes. They must think I'm very strange, wanting to plan them beforehand. Do I try to change it, like a foreigner, or go along with it? Fundraising events do apparently raise large sums of money. A cake sale plus bric-a-brac can bring in anything from £400 to £1,000. Looks like it all works fine as it is.

The other thing that seems 'foreign' is the way people relate to one another when they are in a group. If opinions differ there is no attempt to hide the fact. Indignation is given free rein. Disagreement is voiced strongly. Generally this is not from the men, and definitely not from the English 'blow-ins' of either sex. It's mostly from the women of good Protestant Irish stock. With very firm opinions. But it settles down and the meeting continues.

I guess that was what I saw a hint of last month at the rehearsal for my institution.

June 22 – Saturday

Quite often it feels as if Ireland – or at least this part of it – is about fifty years back in time. This morning at about 9.00 am I drove to the nearest big town to do some shopping. It must have taken about 25 minutes to get there. It was so quiet. In all that time I passed one other vehicle on the road, a small van.

I've been told that the first motorised vehicle in our peninsula was a tractor, in 1974. In 1971 electricity had arrived, though at first only to the more populated areas.

June 24 – Monday

Midsummer Day. Rosie started her job at the restaurant up the road. She had been worried about her visibility walking home after work. But found there was no problem: when she finished at 11.00 pm it was still light.

William the teenager from Canada played the organ in the town church yesterday. He doesn't read music, but plays by ear, so we chose hymns he knew. An interesting mix: 'Amazing grace' ,'Jesus loves me, this I know', and a hymn whose words happened to fit Beethoven's 'Ode to Joy'. Everyone was delighted with him.

I went to the health centre for my monthly magnesium injection. Doctor Larry O'C. was friendly and brisk. When I asked how much I owed him he waved his arm vigorously. 'Get away with you!' he said. I was pleased but puzzled. Afterwards I learnt that the Catholic clergy are never charged so, magnanimously, the Protestant clergy are not either.

In the past I would never have used the word 'Protestant' of myself. In England there are Protestants, Anglicans (Church of England), and Catholics. And whether the Anglicans are Protestant is disputed there. I suppose the word 'Anglican' is too historically sensitive to use in Ireland. Or is it that the Church of Ireland is so 'low church' that they are comfortable being included with members of the Nonconformist Churches such as the Baptists, Presbyterians, Methodists, etc. as 'Protestant'?

June 25 – Tuesday

A rather depressing meeting last night with three members of the Select Vestry (the secretary, the treasurer and one other) to draw up the parish census, which is taken every three years. A lot of it comes down to opinions: 'He *never* comes to church' – 'He does indeed' – and I discovered afterwards that despite what I had been advised locally as to the make-up of the census group, it should have been much larger, with all six churchwardens present. Understandably. But more serious is the number of parishioners who are said to have left the church because of disagreements on one issue or another. Issues of administration rather than theology. I'm told some can perhaps be brought back, others never.

June 26 – Wednesday

I was phoned at 8.15 pm last night by Rose, the secretary of the Select Vestry, to ask if she could give me a lift to the Heritage Centre meeting. There was a small explosion from her when I said I knew nothing about it, hadn't been invited. 'But you're automatically on the committee.' I knew that. Another explosion.

We got to the Centre, which is housed in the former church in the small village midway down the peninsula. This is the church which was shut down four years ago causing much distress. When we went into the building a representative of the local education authority was slightly embarrassed at my not having been invited. It seems it was he who called the meeting, though he is neither secretary nor chairman. 'Not that we wanted to keep anyone out,' he said more than once. 'But I wanted to get things sorted out before ...' Sentence unfinished. Before the new rector saw it all perhaps?

The Centre was started with much enthusiasm by three or four local men, who were advised that to run it there should be a committee with representatives of the church (as lessor of the building) and the local education authority so as to attract grants, and student help during the summer holidays. But it was the local people who were to get the project up and running.

It is difficult to see how they ever thought it could work. Getting items of interest to put into the building was obviously the fun bit for everyone. But then there was to be no entrance charge – 'because it is a church' – and many people still tend the graves that surround the building. Profits for the running of the Centre were to come solely from the sale of refreshments. But there are two pubs in the very small village and two or three food stores. Fundraising events were planned, and some held, but the most recent ones never materialised. Committee members often have not turned up for meetings.

The situation now is that the Centre is considerably in debt: to the bank, to our Select Vestry for rent and insurance, and to two individuals. The educational authority has, not surprisingly, refused the thirty-five year lease that was applied for, until the debts are cleared. If there is no lease the Centre must close, and if it closes

The Famine Church in the distance, seen from Nan's cottage

no money can be made to pay off the debts. The short-term solution would seem to be a one-year lease and some frantic fundraising. And then it closes?

And if the use of the building reverts to the church – to us – I wonder what we do with it?

June 27 – Thursday

Wonderful concert last night in our town church. Part of the West Cork Chamber Music Festival 1996, all other concerts of which are being held in the big town half an hour's drive away. Last night's concert in our church was by the National Chamber Choir from Dublin, with Colin Mawby, whose conducting was totally sensory, sensual, a delight in itself. A mass by Pizzetti (a name I don't know, but I don't know much about music at all) was pure joy. Then there was Palestrina, Monteverdi, Tallis –

Bottom of our avenue ... and the Famine Church

and Mawby. And some amazing modern organ pieces by Fergal Caulfield. The whole concert was bliss.

I had told Francis Humphrys, the dairy farmer whose creation this annual festival is, that I am very much in favour of churches being used for arts events, and he was pleased. If we can have more such events in the future more people will be pleased.

All of which reminds me of a much humbler musical matter. We have begun singing the psalms in our services using a most basic musical pattern. There was, I think, no tradition of singing them in this parish – or hadn't been for some years – and the usual Anglican chant seemed formidable, not least to our regular organist. So, inspired by the training evening we had on May 19, we tried out a very simple way of chanting the first half of the verse on one note except for the final syllable(s), where we go up (or down) a note, and then the second half of the verse on that same chanting note with the final note going up (or down) a little further. As I can't read music I don't know the names of the notes, but I sing them and the organist gallantly copies them from me. She plays them before we begin – just those four notes – and then we sing unaccompanied. It does seem to work, and several people have said they like it. Perhaps it is awful for a really musical ear to hear, I don't know. For the time being it seems worth doing.

Our bedroom in the Rectory faces southwest, in the direction of the Fastnet lighthouse. Going to sleep is accompanied by a gentle sweep of light at the window every five seconds. It somehow reassures that all is well.

June 28 – Friday

A phone call very early this morning from G., a parishioner, asking me to come out to the home of his sister K, because she has killed herself [*date and initials changed for privacy*]. When I arrive at the cottage I walk past the hens and the dog, and the front door is opened by G. He seems very composed. A garda whom I don't know is standing on the far side of the room. K. lies on the earthen floor, having been cut down from the bannisters. I have never attended a suicide before. I had visited K a couple of times – a good woman, with many problems. After a few brief words with G. and the garda, I get out my small purple stole and the oil for anointing, and my prayer book. It feels wrong to stand over her silent body so I kneel down and sit back on my heels, with the two men standing nearby. They join in the prayers where they can. I am aware of a tear or two on my face as I finish but I think there's no harm in that.

G. talks with me, practical matters, and I leave. I guess the doctor will have been the next to arrive.

June 29 – Saturday

I'm trying to put together what I now know about the Revd Mr Fisher and *Tempol na mBocht*, the church that he caused to be built during the great famine of 1847. It seems it is the only Church of Ireland church with an Irish name. He started by setting up soup kitchens in the peninsula, then giving out medicines and clothes and blankets. He raised money from friends in Ireland and England, and began to pay local people to build a school but the response was so great that he decided it should be a church. In the local small town people were dying at the rate of twenty-five a day, whereas in this townland the population decreased during the Famine only from 370 to 343 because of the relief Fisher was providing. He died in 1880 aged 71 of a fever brought on by his work among the sick and dying in a later famine. He had been the Rector of this parish for thirty-eight years.

For Catholics he was a 'souper', his relief work aimed at converting the local people to his church. For Protestants he was a saintly man who cared about the lives of all the people regardless of denomination, at a time when there was no Catholic priest in the peninsula. So they came to him for practical and spiritual support, even for confessions although he tried to dissuade them. In a paper I've been given it was said of him that 'Reverence for holy things was a very marked feature of his religious character: it seemed to underlie everything, for he lived habitually with a sense of the presence of God.'

The following year a charismatic Catholic priest, Archdeacon John Murphy, known from his adventurous youth in Canada as the Black Eagle, came to the peninsula and the Catholics turned back to their original faith.

July 1 – Monday

My morning bellringing is getting worse, not better. If you pull the rope too far down the bell doesn't ring. And of course it also doesn't ring if you don't pull it down far enough. Somewhere in between it rings loud and clear – and then a faint 'ting' sometimes follows, which spoils the sound pattern completely. But I don't know why. I wish I could *see* the bell from where I stand below.

Twice now I've had people join me for Morning Prayer and meditation. Once it was a parishioner whose aunt had just died. I was glad she wanted to come: that felt good. And one day last week it was a tourist. I'd seen the motor caravan parked in the lay-by outside the church and wondered whether the bell-ringing would be a nasty shock for whoever was inside it. But ten minutes later someone came in, genuflected (a Catholic?) and sat down. I gave her a book and she very happily joined me in saying the Franciscan form of morning prayer that some Anglican clergy are now using. Afterwards we had a brief, pleasant chat.

More visiting today. I met Ken, a retired English widower – a lovely kind and gentle man but I could *not* persuade him to call me anything but 'Canon'. He told me some nice things about my predecessor. Getting a sense of what this person I have never met is like is fascinating and gets built up from many differing accounts. Ken also said that the congregation of the church he goes to, our town church, is ready to move forward in terms of liturgy and music, and that I will not find much opposition. Or that any opposition would be from a very small number. Which is good to know.

Then I drove out to the third church, the summer church, St Brendan's. It is in such a perfect setting, on a rocky spit of land with a natural harbour on its north side, and the sea a short distance away on the south side. Its graveyard runs down to the edge of the harbour water. It has a beautiful bare stone interior, and if lighting is needed it is by gas – and it will be with that lovely soft 'perrr-lop!' when a match is applied to the mantle.

The first of the summer evening services is due to take place there this coming Sunday. I have only ever been in the building once before, during my interview day. I was pleased to find the door wide open – and horrified to find dust and cobwebs everywhere. There is supposed to be a group of young people cleaning the church and cutting the long grass in the graveyard this week, but there is no sign of their presence and I have had no notification of their coming to do it.

To tea with a farm family in the evening-afternoon. On the way there I drove out along a lane I had not explored before (though there are still a great many of them). On the map it went straight along beside a steep hill and stopped among clifftop fields. Somewhere here was the house of B., who a month ago celebrated her 100th birthday

'The stone church at the end of the peninsula', St Brendan's

and got a telegram from President Mary Robinson, and £300. At the end of the lane I found a seascape-landscape of wild beauty, the sea turning from deep blue and green into a huge expanse of foaming whiteness as it met the rocks. And this was a pleasant summer day. What is it like in rough weather?

At the farm I was given a tour by Jennifer, the farmer's wife. I had previously, as a onetime Norfolk smallholder with a few cows and sheep, expressed curiosity about the way silage is made and stored in this part of wet Ireland. Most hay here is indeed made into silage as there is generally too much rain for it to be baled in any quantity. I was shown the barn-sized covered pit, where the hay is piled up, with molasses spread on it at intervals, for feeding the sixty cattle that are wintered in the adjoining

Drawing of St Brendan's, by Brian Lalor

buildings. In a further yard was another pit, almost as large, but without a roof. Instead, the silage was covered with black polythene and car tyres. Away in a distant field we could see the two farmer brothers turning the hay to make square bales which they would then sell. If it went well there would be a thousand bales from that field and they would get a good price. They keep no bales for their own use: they use only silage.

Another view of St Brendan's

We went back into the farmhouse. I had been given tea (and cakes) at the farm on a previous visit. But this was real tea, such as I remember fondly from rural Wales in the 1940s. The whole extended family, children and adults, sat down together for salad, which was lettuce and tomatoes and cucumber and beetroot and sliced hard-boiled eggs, with sliced ham and bread and butter and scones and fruit tart and sponge cake and cups and cups of tea. The only difference from the Welsh teas of the 1940s was that the sponge cake here, now, did not have plain jam as a filling but whipped cream and strawberries. Everything was so homely in its presentation and so beautifully made. This is a well-to-do farming family with a fitted pine kitchen. The younger children cluster shyly but readily around me, showing me a great number of family photographs. The eldest girl, in her late teens, looks on with a gentle and amused detachment. I search for what it is she reminds me of, and then realise. She is fresh out of Jane Austen.

July 2 – Tuesday

A parishioner has offered to buy a photocopier for the parish – as long as the donation can be anonymous. Another person wants to provide wheelchair access to the town church, in memory of his wife who was disabled, but turns down the idea of even a small memorial plaque. That the new access existed would be memorial enough, he says. Another person wants to replace with proper locks some unsightly padlocks on the external doors of St Brendan's, the far west stone church. Two or three others want to pay to improve audibility in that same church. Three people came to me after leaving a church hall to say that between them they would put up an outdoor halogen light, if I was amenable. Someone I visited recently asked if he could give me a cheque, if there was anything that was needed.

All of which is odd, in a parish that is heavily in debt. Or *is* it odd? It suggests that even where there are people who have money, they prefer to do something concrete with it, rather than pay

Drawing of window at St Brendan's by Brian Lalor

it into what is seen as a bottomless diocesan coffer. Very human. Maybe the churches could learn to go along with that sort of sentiment? In a congregationalist way? I'm not sure it would be comfortable for the clergy to know which ten or twenty people were paying their stipend – or good for the ten or twenty to know it, either!

The group of young Canadians, including William the Inuit lad who played the organ for us last week, are going to paint and generally renovate our main parish hall in a few hours' concentrated work by all thirty of them. Their leader, Ken, asked if there was any sort of community project they could undertake while they were here, and that was what was decided on. Wonderful!

But there is no news concerning the cleaning of St Brendan's for this Sunday. The Select Vestry meeting was adamant that it was done annually and automatically, along with the grass cutting of the graveyard, by 'the youth group from the diocese.' But the diocesan office knows nothing about a youth group, and could only suggest I phone the Church Army man, as being most likely to know of one. I can't reach him by phone. We could get a work party together from this end of the parish to clean out the church, since there are very few parishioners in that little harbour village where the church is, but we are running short of time. It seems that it wasn't automatic at all, but something that my predecessor arranged year by year. I wish he had left a contact number.

July 3 – Wednesday

Cold and windy. But our washing machine is functioning at last, thanks to Billy's vast DIY skills. And the house is looking fine, with pictures finally up on the walls due to days of John's blasting through stone with the electric drill. Domestic life is such a pleasure. I could be like Parson Woodforde, in his eighteenth century diary, and list all our meals? Rosie and John and I all take turns with the cooking. When Rosie lived in her own flat in Norwich there was only John and me to share meals preparation, so three is a bonus. And although here the exotic foods we used then are either unavailable or generally too expensive for us, the basics are very good. Today's lunch is brown soda bread, with that gorgeous acidity; and wonderful white bread made from unbleached flour in an ancient brick oven in a shop in the town; local butter; and a local cheese that is now exported all over the world, made by two of our parishioners, and bought in the town from a great variety of Irish cheeses. And homegrown lettuce and shallots given to us by a parishioner, with a promise of jam from her incredibly laden blackcurrant bushes.

I forgot to write in last weekend that Rosie and I went exploring the land beyond the garden. We know that in all there are thirty-three acres of it. At first we were climbing between bushes and small trees and brambles on otherwise bare soil but we soon reached the tree-line and we could see the sky again, above a great expanse of gorse. It is difficult to force your way through because the ground is so uneven and sometimes the next step lurches you downwards, in it to knee-height. We must bring walking sticks next time. At one place we found a drystone wall, almost out of sight among the gorse, winding its way downhill. So this must at some time have

View from the cairn behind the Rectory

been grazing land. We went on climbing up. We had each
brough a stone with us because Nan had said there was a
cairn at the top and that if we got there we must add to it.

We got there. I've no idea how long it took. Yes, there
was a cairn, about five feet high, and we added our stones
to it. But the best thing was the view. All out across the
bay and out, out to the open Atlantic.

July 4 – Thursday

A phone call this evening from Hugh, the church
glebewarden, to say that the Canadians have finished
painting and repairing the parish hall, and to ask would I
go along with him tomorrow evening to the backpackers'
hostel where they are all staying. He wants to thank them
and give them a huge box of chocolates and wish them
well for the Atlantic Challenge that they go off to on

Saturday, competing against similar young sailing teams from other countries.

And a parishioner from the harbour village where St Brendan's is has phoned to say that although she is now too old to help clean the church out, she has got together a working party of villagers to do it, and I am not to worry, it will be fine. My thanks were certainly heartfelt.

In the evening John and I had a splendid time in what has become our favourite bar in the town. 'Traditional music', the handwritten notice on the window says most Thursdays. But for Dave and Venetia, who run the place, that doesn't mean performances but 'sessions', with the musicians sitting in a circle around one of the tables and playing essentially for each other, with the bar customers listening or not, applauding or not – that's very secondary. It is great.

July 5 – Friday

9.30 am: have just been told by one of the Canadian team that William has been very seriously injured in a road accident.

Later: William is on a life-support system in Cork Hospital, and not responding. I've been at the hostel here, with the young people (who were at first not aware how serious his condition is) and Ken, the group's leader. Will had been cycling down a road the other side of the town from the hostel, early this morning during an exercise period, and was in collision with a car. Tragically his instinctive Canadian road sense made him swerve to the right to avoid it rather than to the left. His skull is fractured. This Sunday is his sixteenth birthday. The group is due to move on to Bantry tomorrow, but Ken and the other leaders want to consult with the whole group before deciding whether to go or to stay on in this place where they had all got to know each other. Even if they go to Bantry, Ken says, they will come back to us for the Sunday morning service, whatever the developments.

I tried to contact Father Hurley because some of the young people are Catholics and had been going to Mass on Sundays, but he is on holiday. I must get in touch with the further-west Parish Priest.

July 6 – Saturday

The news from the hospital chaplain is that Will is still alive. He has survived the first crucial twenty-four hours but has serious brain damage. His parents were granted an immediate visa and are expected from Canada soon.

July 8 – Monday

A prayer vigil is being arranged: a half hour of said prayers and a reading and moments of silent prayer. We hear that Will is to be brought off the life support system today, so this is a crucial time. His chances are 50-50. His parents are now with him. Father Hurley is still away but the priest from further down the peninsula, who is covering for him, is very willing to be involved in the vigil. So I took A4 notices all around the town and got a dozen into strategic shops with no trouble at all. Everyone has heard of William. I went the length of the street and around to the convent and when I walked back up the street a few minutes later all the notices were up in the shop windows. And this was on a busy Monday morning with the place full of tourist shoppers.

July 9 – Tuesday

About fifty people came to the vigil in our church last night, including some of the nuns from the convent. Today there are new notices around the town, announcing that a fund to pay for accommodation for Will's parents has been set up and can be paid into the bank. Everyone asks about him, grieves for his parents.

Early August

Now we've been here two months. Time, I guess, to stop this 'public' diary. It can't go on for ever as there must be a limit to how much small print can be read by family and friends. It was all those first impressions that I wanted to catch and convey, and they are fading now as events and observations become familiar and cease to startle.

William is still alive. I was able to see him in the ICU in hospital in Cork, and to meet his devastated parents, Johnnie and Nancy. Will is due to be flown back to Canada with them as I write this. But his chances of survival are not high. Decisions must now be made about the disbursement of the remainder of the 'William Fund', which the town's Development Association have asked me to administer.

Rosie is still seeing her fisherman, Richie, whom we like very much. There is said to be some disapproval of him in the town for going out with 'a Protestant', even though she is in fact agnostic. 'This is medieval,' she storms quietly. It may be only one young man who is causing this trouble, though, a known IRA supporter. All the same, we are slightly shocked.

The wonderful summer Sunday evening services have been happening at the little stone church at the end of the peninsula. It is small but always almost full of parishioners from the other two churches, but also of local villagers of all denominations or none, and summer tourists ditto. The pattern is that we have the traditional end-of-day service of Compline, and a sermon by a visiting preacher, who may be a retired bishop, or a local Catholic priest, or – planned – a Jewish rabbi who has a holiday home here. The visiting preachers have been a joy.

Friends and family have been to visit or stay with us, and more are planning to come to this 'foreign country'.

We have new Irish registration plates for our car.

This place feels like home.

Autumn 1996

It's no good. I can't not do this diary. Too much happens that I want to record. There's a big gap. But I'll just have to re-start it.

August 14 – Wednesday

Today I went to the very small village halfway down the peninsula, to send a fax to the regional newspaper about the closing down of the 'William Fund'. We have agreed to transfer the money to Atlantic Challenge in Canada to administer for the accommodation of Will's parents and sister in Montreal. That is where he is in hospital now, still in a coma, but we've been told there is a slight improvement. As the fund was only an ad hoc local one we don't have to satisfy any equivalent of the Charity Commissioners about sending it or closing down the account. There is still £2,350 in it, even after £450 has already been paid out to Nancy and Johnnie, Will's parents.

Then I went to see Jackie because I realise he hasn't been at church for two Sundays. I checked with Nan in the Post Office first, that he isn't away. No, but she too had noticed he wasn't there on Sunday. He is getting very forgetful, she says. and capable of not remembering that it was Sunday. So I go to his small old farmhouse, taking from Nan a magazine he had ordered.

I've never visited him at home before, but have had many long chats with him, chats which usually involved a lot of repetition on his part. The farmhouse which is so very neat and well-painted seen from the front, is drab and forlorn at the back. The huge black-rolled bales that fill his yard must have been made by whoever farms his land now. His familiar rusty car is not in evidence.

The kitchen door knocker has become immoveable with age. But tapping produces Jackie, unshaven, alarmed eyes, and 'Who is it?' I reassure him, and he becomes soft and instantly begins his usual conversation about his wife's death last year. He is a good man, and has been a pillar of the church in his time, reading the lessons and even starting services by pre-arrangement if the clergy were to be late in arriving. I normally only see him on Sundays when he is beautifully turned out in his best clothes. Now he is touched that I have come to see if he is all right – yes, he is – and full of wonder that I have been able to find his house. We talk a while, out in a sunny yard circled by small trees. He asks about the Rectory, and whether I like it, and whether the man who lives there with me likes it also. He tells me he can hear every word I say in church (he often tells me that) and that there is no reason why women should not be rectors, if they have a message to give. When I eventually drive away he doesn't go back into his empty house but stays in the yard, waving. A dear man.

That expression he used, 'if they have a message to give,' has a Non-Conformist ring to it. I've heard it used in England by Methodists. I know the Methodists had a church here in the peninsula: I've seen it in one of the out of the way townlands, overgrown but still standing. I imagine Jackie was a member of it, years ago. So too, probably, was another parishioner, now very old and very ill, who always asks when I visit him and his wife, if I would like him to close with prayer. And he does, at considerable length, a beautiful long and very devout conversation with God on behalf of the three of us. Another former Methodist, I am sure. I will ask next time I see him.

From Jackie's I went to call in on Kathleen, a small smiling woman who runs a large market garden of organic vegetables. And another Kathleen, who I had been seeing at the nursing home in the town until it was closed two weeks ago. She went from there to a larger home, attached to the hospital of a town many miles away, and there was a lot of sadness around the parish about that. When I called there a week later to see her I was told she'd just gone home – to her daughter's, not far from the Rectory. Wonderful. She looks better than I've ever seen her. She is delighted when I ask if she has her prayer books with her – she hasn't, so I say I'll bring some – and also delighted when I offer to get her books from the library regularly ('I can't understand people who don't read at all'). And then even more delighted when I offer to arrange a lift to church for her on Sundays. She was another pillar of the church, leading bible study groups and always ready to fill in with reading lessons and other duties at short notice. Now her voice is very soft, and her broad smile is beautiful. A holy lady.

It has been a beautiful day, sunny from the beginning. The washing was out on the line at 7.30 am!

August 16 – Friday

A meeting of the Select Vestry last night. And despite having been told that no agenda is needed, so that items could be put in at the last minute, or left out if that seemed better, I presented members with a typed agenda. Some were clearly pleased with the development. During the meeting I suggested that if the minutes could be typed then copies could be circulated soon after the meeting, and they would then not need to be read out at the start of the next meeting. But the Secretary said she had been told it was a legal requirement that the minutes be handwritten to avoid falsification. This cannot be true, not even in Ireland, in the 1990s. Before this meeting I had not had sight of the minutes of the previous meeting, which are normally only written the day before the next meeting. I must talk to someone at the diocesan office.

August 18 – Sunday

Afternoon: I am sitting in the dining room, sewing, with BBC Radio 4 on. I am listening to J. M. Synge's *The Aran Islands*, about the cruelty of the sea and the poor drowned fisherman and the lovely girl from Aran whom the protagonist couldn't somehow imagine in his Dublin-and-Paris life – and in the next room Rosie is laughing and talking with Richie, who tells droll stories about his fishing life and his brother, also a fisherman, and others who have nearly drowned.

Later: Have had a phone call from the village at the end of the peninsula, where we had a service this evening. An 18-year-old girl has fallen off the pier and drowned.

August 20 – Tuesday

The Diocesan Secretary is puzzled that anyone should think that Select Vestry minutes had to be handwritten. So I talked to the SV Secretary, suggesting that this part of her work could be greatly reduced if at the end of each meeting she gives me a note of any voting, and any financial figures given etc., that I could produce as minutes on the word processor and give out copies to members, especially absent ones, and then the minutes would not have to be read aloud at the next meeting, taking up unnecessary time. But she says she would like to keep up the old way as it is so lovely to read the old books going back over the years. It's touching, really.

A nasty incident last weekend. Rosie and Richie now spend every Friday and Saturday evening together in the town, and all day every Sunday here at the Rectory. On Saturday, in a very crowded bar, one of the men there said to Richie – presumably quietly – something unpleasant about Richie and 'the Rector's daughter'. Richie said the man was very drunk at the time. All the same, it is another indication that not everything here is sweetness and light.

August 21 – Wednesday

I had been asked to call in on Audrey, an Anglo-Irish woman. So I went to visit her today. A long drive down a winding lane, then up a winding boreen, and then my way was blocked by a farm gate with a notice: 'Beware the bull .' But adding in a more kindly tone 'Please shut this gate after you'. Assuming the bull was fictional I went through: and then found myself driving up a steep and sideways-sloped grassy pathway on the side of a field. If I hadn't been able to see the house I'd have thought I was in the wrong place altogether.

The small old farmhouse stands on the top of a knoll, peeping out of small back windows at a wonderful view of rocks and sea. There were a few outbuildings, and a few derelict remains of some old buildings but otherwise the house stands proud. The front of it, which you have to walk around to, opens out hospitably into a pretty little garden. What an amazing place for an old lady to live in on her own. No car though. I knocked, walked about, banged, waited. She wasn't in. I left a card. I shall have to go back another day. Good.

And then there was the cake sale, back in the town, in our parish hall. Several Catholic women were helping with it. I had been told this happened – and that it is reciprocated when there is a fund-raising event at the Catholic church. It's about the most hopeful thing I've encountered, ecumenically speaking. Father Hurley, the town Parish Priest, is friendly but the other PP in this area is rather reserved. I understand he is not pro-ecumenism.

Although he did take part in the vigil in our church for the Inuit lad after his accident.

Considering that ecumenism, and hope for it in this country, was one of the things that brought me here I have done very little about it; feeling I suppose that I need to get my bearings. But my bearings such as they are at this stage aren't very strong. The Methodists, east of our parish, are small in number but very friendly. There are no other denominations in the area, though I'm told the Quakers from Cork have a special day on one of the islands in the summer. I have been trying to get some information from the Irish Council of Churches and the Council of Churches for Britain and Ireland about ecumenical events, or publications, etc. without much success. I've also been asking if there are any shared church buildings in Ireland. It's a great shame that our wonderful stone church at the end of the peninsula is only used on Sunday evenings in July and August, even though it is in a small village with a lot of tourists in the summer. There are only three Church of Ireland people in that village, but a lot of Catholics of course. And no Catholic church. The Catholics go back down the peninsula to the middle village. But the Parish Priest of that area is the one who is said to be anti-ecumenism. So no hope there, I guess.

August 23 – Friday

Wednesday's cake sale raised £342. And was generally enjoyed, I think, with everybody working and chatting together.

We've been sent a copy of a big feature piece in the English newspaper the *Independent on Sunday*. 'Forget Tuscany,' it says, 'forget the Dordogne: the place to be is West Cork.' And lists some of the famous people who live here or have second homes here. Rosie is goggle-eyed when Mary the bookshop owner says that Jeremy Irons was in her bookshop recently. Even I get a *frisson* from the thought that I might have seen Jeremy Paxman around.

Rosie has given up her job at the restaurant and found a cottage to rent in the small town. It's good that she is no longer dependant on us or Richie to provide transport for her.

August 24 – Saturday

A lovely day. Richie took Matthew and Rosie and me in to the island where his family have a few pieces of land.

At the pier with the island in the distance

Walking onto the island (top) and the former school

It was great to be on the water, in the sunshine, then mooring at the pier. Not many people live on the island these days, not more than a dozen, though as recently as thirty years ago, Richie says, there were more than fifty.

At the pier there were a couple of rather battered old cars and a van. No driving licences needed here, and no vehicle checks. The roads are rough tracks, and land that must have in the past supported families is now mostly overgrown. Some cows amble around what used to be the schoolhouse. We cut off the track into some lumpy, gorse-filled ground, and plough our way towards a cut in the south cliff and down into the inlet. We can hear water flowing downwards towards the sea. Then we see it, gushing out of the rock. There is a tin mug hanging on a string nearby. Richie rinses it, fills it, hands it to me.

It is the most beautiful water I have ever, ever tasted. There are no words for it. The best I can do is that the experience of it was bliss, pure bliss.

August 26 – Monday

The Bishop was at the far west stone church yesterday, our final visiting preacher there for the summer. He and Mrs W stayed overnight with us at the Rectory. He is a dear, and she is nicely sparky, so it was all pleasantly enjoyable.

And I met Audrey at St B's, the woman who had not been at home in her delightful cottage when I called last week. She came and introduced herself to me. I really don't know why I had been expecting an old woman. She is spiritedly young!

Oh, but there have been so many accidents and tragedies here this summer. First William's road accident; then last Sunday I got the phone call from the far west village to say that a teenage girl had been killed by falling backwards off the harbour wall. Then on the Monday a woman died on the other side of the peninsula while fishing on a rock with her husband: a freak wave washed her off the rock and she was drowned. The same week four young children were caught by the under currant at a nearby bay and nearly drowned: one took nearly an hour to resuscitate. All were taken by two ambulances to Bantry hospital, with our local doctor going with them.

August 27 – Tuesday

This afternoon I did a home Communion service for a housebound parishioner. Not for the first time, but previously it has been in her drawing room. This time she was in bed. I suggested we had the service first and then I could go and make tea for both of us. Fine. So I put on my small stole, and set up my 'travelling' silver cup and plate, with the bread and wine. I gave her the prayer sheet, and we began. We were about halfway through when she asked if I could stop for a minute and pass her the bedpan. Which I did, and which she used. I then removed the pan, washed my hands, and we resumed the service. And had a nice cup of tea afterwards.

August 28 – Wednesday

John and I were told a few days ago that someone we know and like here – not a parishioner but a social friend – is said to be a member of the IRA. We keep telling ourselves that this is only a rumour, but it is stunning how we have subtly reassessed that person now in our minds. Can't believe it, one half of the mind says. But of course, why not, the other half says. We are probably very gullible.

Two people today have told me – quite separately – that tragic events destroyed their belief in God. One was after the Great War ('When I saw what people could do to other people') and the other after her husband died ('He was such a good man'). It is so common – and so sad – to lose faith in God in such situations. But to blame *God* for the inhumanity of *people* seems to me illogical. In the other case, the illogicality seems to be to believe that one particular person should live indefinitely – or at least be guaranteed to live until after you have died (thereby putting *them* through the hell of bereavement), simply because they are the person you love. Perhaps, especially in bereavement, their grief and depression is so deep that any sense they had of God gets lost. Are we, as a Church, failing to encourage a life-giving relationship with God?

Talking of depression, there are so many depressed elderly women here, mostly from the farms, many of them having to go to one or other of the local psychiatric hospitals from time to time. I can't help wondering if there is a cause common to most of them: but this is delicate ground to venture into without any more than basic counselling training. Yet it worries me that as far as I can tell the only help they are getting in hospital is medication.

August 29 – Thursday

'Is the minister there?' the phone caller asked Rosie.

'No, she's out.'

'Are you his wife then?'

'No, you want my mother. She's not here now but she'll be back soon.'

'What?'

'My mother is the minister.'

'Oh.'

August 30 – Friday

People here have a strong built-in sense of direction. They tend to say 'I'm going north tomorrow' even when it's just the next town. Or 'She moved east,' instead of naming the town or area. And today a farmer told me that a new house was being built 'just east here' – meaning a little way along the lane – and another house, she said is to be built soon 'in the field, west'. A retired teacher told me that a small boy, chided for the back of his neck being grubby, said that he couldn't reach it, it was 'too far west'. (Cottages usually face east.)

But it's a valuable instinct to develop, I guess, in an area where it must be easy to get lost, with the mists coming down the sides of the hills thick and white, even on a day in August!

August 31 – Saturday

We met Richie's family this afternoon. His mother, Margaret, is local born and bred, devoutly Catholic. She met his father, Johnnie, when she was an *au pair* in New York. He is Italian American, but they have all lived here since Richie was two years old. Richie has three brothers and a sister. So, four boys and a girl, just like us. Margaret doesn't go out much but Johnnie is always joking and seems to know and be known by everyone in the town.

It's a very different world for Rosie to be getting into.

September 3 – Tuesday

Rosie has been in the Mercy hospital in Cork for the last couple of days with suspected appendicitis. She came out today: she's okay. She was amazed at how Catholic everything in the hospital was: the statues, the holy water stoups, and even the ward round of Holy Communion, brought by a nun. She had great difficulty persuading the nun that she shouldn't, as a good Protestant agnostic, have it.

September 5 – Thursday

I've never given much thought to the famine church's font. It is slim, and simple, and pleasant to look at but with very little detail on it. Now I have information about it that has delighted me. Nan said once that it had come from one of the local islands, but I had not remembered which one. Apparently it was from Cape Clear Island, which we have been to once, by a plunging and leaping ferry. It is a small *Gaeltacht*, an Irish-speaking area. And it is where St Ciarán (a.k.a. Kieran) was born, who is said to be the earliest of Ireland's four saints who brought Christianity to this country, probably in the fourth century, before St Patrick arrived in the fifth century. What the four saints spread was a very Celtic Christianity, which absorbed the ancient myths and heroes, whereas the religion which Patrick brought was from Rome. Our lovely font is from the fourteenth or fifteenth century, and must have come from the twelfth century church, the ruins of which I believe can still be seen. I want to go back there.

September 6 – Friday

Rosie and Richie got engaged today. They bought the ring in Skibbereen this afternoon, and this evening his mother and father, and uncle Connie who is a priest in Nigeria but home on holiday, came over for smoked salmon and 'champagne' – and speeches! We're all very happy.

September 8 – Sunday

Now we've been here four months. Soon I'll forget to count.

September 9 – Monday

Visiting an elderly couple, out in the middle of a tangle of farm lanes. A grassy yard, a traditional cottage. The small room that the front door opens into is dark, and my eyes slowly adjust to it. Gradually I see an old range, a square table, three chairs. At the tiny window one shutter is open. I see a long wooden settle, put against a staircase that rises from the darkness to an upper level.

The hospitality is very kind. On the table is a new teapot, one china cup and saucer, and an array of bread, butter, biscuits and cake. I am asked to pull my chair up to the table. They will have theirs later, they say. Good gentle people, moving without hurry in their heavy farm boots. Kindly and intelligent. Yet the woman has only ever been to Cork city once. The man quotes a long passage of scripture to me – and then asks a sharp question about it. I would like to pursue it further than we do, only his local accent is so strong that I am not always sure of what he is saying.

How can I preach to and for good people like this when I don't know what is in their heads, what they are thinking? And how can I preach to and for people like this and *also* the sophisticated lawyers and financiers spending weekends in their elegant holiday homes?

September 10 – Tuesday

I have started teaching at the Community College. Every week I am to have three separate classes in just under two hours: twelve year olds to fourteen year olds. The Church of Ireland students separate out from their classmates when 'Religion' is on the timetable, and they come to me. Me, without any teacher training, and with no curriculum. I am to teach them. Poor kids. But nice, all of them. We get through the first morning very amiably.

The educational system here is interesting. There is a 'transition year' when the students are about fourteen, in which they get a taste of the working world. They and their parents or guardians find them someone engaged in business or farming or hospitality, etc., who will take them on as unpaid apprentices for the year. This will be part-time, mixed with standard subjects back at the college. I think it is brilliant. It is an experience of the reality of future employment, whether or not they stay in the occupation they have chosen for that year.

September 11 – Wednesday

One of my parishioners, elderly and rather grand, had been worrying people by her driving habits. Her ancient car was often to be seen parked in the village with one front wheel well up onto the footpath. And in the road if you saw her coming the other way you'd be wise to pull over and let her pass in her own time. But I hadn't seen her in town for a while and went to visit her a few days ago. Her car was in its place beside the house. Over bone china teacups she told me there was something wrong with the car and that B., from the garage, couldn't find what the problem was, so now she has to get neighbours to drive her to the village. I have since found out what the problem was. The doctor, the garda, her niece and B., who were all worried about her, got together about it and B. removed a vital part from the motor. Problem solved.

September 14 – Saturday

To Dublin, for Richard Clarke's consecration as Bishop of the Diocese of Meath and Kildare. Richard has until now been the Dean of Cork. He was one of the four or five people who interviewed me in the Deanery six months ago. Today's service was beautiful. When people like Richard are made bishops there is hope for the Church.

September 15 – Sunday

Our Harvest Thanksgiving service. Father Hurley is our guest preacher. Flattered to be asked, he said – because the Catholics don't have harvest festivals! The tea afterwards is in the now-lovely Rectory, to show it off for the first official time to the parishioners, who have of course been paying for it.

September 16 – Monday

To Cork in the evening to give a talk on contemplative prayer to the Mothers' Union. Two weeks ago I did a

Quiet Day on the same subject in the Cathedral. I am hoping a small group or two might be started.

September 17 – Tuesday

Teaching again at the Community College. I am enjoying putting together some sort of curriculum for each of the three classes I take.

And I am very impressed by the atmosphere in the college. Although the students' ages range from eleven to eighteen there is no rowdyism, they move about chatting normally to each other – and to the staff. You can see a young person walking down a corridor and a staff member coming the other way, and they will stop for a minute and exchange a few words as if they were each a normal human being, and move on. – I had to see the Principal in his office about some papers, and told him how impressed I was. He said it has been like that from the earliest days of the college. The first thing a new pupil has to sign up to when they start at the college is 'Respect for others'.

But it is like that on the public buses also. School-children get on with a 'hello' to the driver when they board, and a 'goodbye' when they get off. I wonder how much of it is tradition and how much is because there's probably a chance that the one is a five-times-removed cousin of the other. A bit of both, probably.

September 20 – Friday

To Castletownbeare, an hour and a half away, to preach at the Harvest Thanksgiving service there. I was very much looking forward to going because it was when we were on holiday and passed through there that I was horrified to see a padlocked Church of Ireland church; and the first sense of a call to Ireland touched me. It is a lovely fishing town. But for all sorts of reasons I think I am better placed where I am working now.

September 23 – Monday

We have had a stream of family and friends staying with us this summer and autumn, and have enjoyed every minute of their visits, and mourned their departures. Distance makes the heart grow more aware of how precious these relationships are, and in most cases how much better, richer, they get as we all mature.

October 2 – Wednesday

I dial Betty's number. 'Hello Billy. Is Betty there?'

'Betty is not there. I'll get her for you.'

The language here still startles us occasionally with its differences. And still sometimes leads us into misunderstandings. Talk of a 'ditch' around one of the churchyards puzzled me until it was pointed out that here a ditch is anything that keeps livestock out. So it can go down, like an English ditch, or up – it can be a hedge or a wall.

Although this peninsula is not an Irish speaking area a certain amount of Irish words slip into conversation sometimes. Like *flaithiúl* (pronounced 'fla*hool*),' for generous. And *plámás* (pronounced 'plaw*mauce*') meaning to flatter in order to get what you want. Sometimes you hear *sin scéal eile* ('shin shkale ella') – that's another story.

October 5 – Saturday

No funerals in the parish for five months – and then suddenly two in one week. A ninety-six year old woman on Monday, and a man of ninety on Friday. One from the farming community, the other ex-Colonial English: neither of them was one of our parishioners. Funerals are very different here. For one thing, they are usually held three days after the death, instead of the seven day gap that is normal in England. And there are more happenings, more rituals connected with the death, no matter whether the deceased is Catholic or Protestant or other. The priest or minister will often have been present at the death or soon after, and there will be prayers, usually with family members and perhaps neighbours.

*Communal graveyard by the ruins of the
original Church of Ireland church*

Communal graveyard

The next stage is the Removal next day to the funeral home in the town, which often looks almost like a shop. Now the community is involved. People from all the surrounding area will come in, walk up to the open coffin and stand in silence for a few moments, the Catholics crossing themselves. From the very old to babies or toddlers carried by their parents, none shows any disquiet in gazing down at the still face in the coffin. They have been doing this since before they can remember.

Then they circle around the coffin and pass along the line of closest family members, shaking hands and saying the traditional 'Sorry for your loss,' mostly fairly solemnly and formally: but sometimes hugs or kisses are exchanged. The long line moves on, out onto the pavement to allow others to come in. This can go on for an hour or two, with maybe a couple of hundred people coming in.

Finally, the priest or minister will begin a short service of readings and prayers, everyone standing, and with the doors open and the words relayed by PA to the silent crowd outside. Then all leave except the immediate family and the priest. The doors are closed. The funeral director asks the family to make their farewells. These minutes, just before the coffin is sealed, are often the time when grief is most openly felt and expressed, as family members touch or kiss the loved one for the last time and turn away into each other's arms. A prayer is said as the lid is screwed down; the doors are opened again.

The bearers – family members if possible – lift the coffin on to their shoulders. They carry it out into the street and, led by the priest and followed by the silent crowd, they walk the few yards to the Catholic church in one direction or the Church of Ireland church in the other direction. One or more members of the gardaí is on duty to halt the traffic. Shops close their doors and turn their lights off as the procession passes.

Reception in the church is the next stage. The crowd will have thinned but nevertheless a good number follow the coffin into the building, where more prayers are said. Then the coffin is left there for the night.

The next day there is the funeral service with invariably a full church and sometimes a crowd outside. There will be as many people at the funeral as at the removal, but not all the same people. For some, a 7.00 pm removal is easier to get to than a 3.00 pm funeral: for others the opposite. Family or friends will read a passage of scripture, or sing, or play a short piece of music, or give a eulogy. In the Catholic church people bring forward items that represent the life of the deceased – a photo, a hurley stick, even a mobile phone – and place them on the coffin.

Finally another walking procession, this time to the communal graveyard down the road, overlooking the harbour, and there the interment takes place. People break away into groups and chat as they walk back towards the hotel or one of the town bars where some or all have been invited for refreshments.

October 9 – Wednesday

To Bandon yesterday to do another Harvest preachment. I think all these invites must be because I'm new to the diocese. Bandon is an hour and a half's drive from here through the now familiar landscape of the road to Cork, but in beautiful sunshine and even, at one stage, a stunning rain-and-sun rainbow. Rain and sun happen so much and so often here that it no longer elicits our amazement: but it *is* lovely.

Patrick Comerford, of the *Irish Times*, phoned this evening with depressing news. As I had been seeing quite a few pieces by him in various publications, and then discovered he is a Diocesan Reader in the Church of Ireland, I had put on paper to him the case for a new newspaper covering all the churches in Ireland. And had spoken between the lines, I hoped, about the inadequacies of present provision. But he says it has been tried – and failed. It was about four years ago, he thinks, that a group of people ran an ecumenical paper for a short time. His analysis of its failure is that church people are rigidly loyal to their existing papers. Even if they are atrocious (my words, not his).

I'm not sure I'm convinced. The last time I was told 'No, it's been tried – and failed,' was from an English Archbishop when I proposed an ecumenical network of contemplative prayer groups. But one failure should not mean 'never again'. In that case, persistence paid off and the result was a network of about 400 ecumenical groups all over Britain.

October 11 – Friday

Diocesan Synod yesterday. A lot of people there asked if it was very different from what I was used to in England. The representation is different: all the diocesan clergy were there, in Cork, and our parish has a good number of lay representatives. The business was different in that this Synod meets only once a year, and it lasts all day, from 11.00 am (after a 9.45 am Eucharist attended by nearly all, even though some have had to drive for more than two hours to get there) and included a big restaurant-style lunch, through to 4.30 pm tea. Yet it consisted mainly of reports of various councils such as healing, or youthwork, or stewardship. Each of these reports was spoken to, sometimes fairly lengthily, before being accepted. So there was no room on the agenda for a single major item of current concern. On the other hand it does ensure that people are aware of what is happening in these areas: if they had to wait to see them in the annual diocesan report they probably wouldn't get to read most of them. None of those councils have any fulltime staff:

but then, there are only twenty-nine clergy in the diocese, including four who are auxiliary (unpaid). Ten retired clergy have permission to officiate, and there are twenty-two Lay Readers, one of whom is in charge of a parish.

It was good to get a few minutes' chat here and there with other clergy. Most of us are very isolated in our work. I've been guest preacher this year at four other parishes's Harvest Thanksgiving services in September and October – people generally swap around for this so I have met some others during these two months. But for most of the year the only contact seems to be the monthly 'Clerical', arranged for the clergy of this part of the diocese by an elderly retired priest. But that consists of *two* talks by two pre-arranged speakers. All very academic, with almost no time for chat and exchange of news and views. There is a mild rebellion building up about this. I am not the only one who feels the need for an unstructured meeting time. But people are so polite to each other, and no-one wants to hurt the feelings of the retired priest.

October 12 – Saturday

John has won second prize in a short story competition organised by UCC [University College Cork] Radio. Proof to him that you don't have to be Irish to get anywhere here with your writing.

Our third son Matthew has phoned from Norwich to say he is now sure he wants to move here. Hopes to be with us before Christmas. Since Rosie has now moved to a cottage of her own in the town we have a spare room for him. It seems possible that he could make a decent living for himself as a gardener.

October 14 – Monday

I visit Lizzie again in B. hospital's new psychiatric unit, to take Holy Communion to her. Her depression seems, if anything, worse than it was a month ago. As far as I can make out she is getting no psychotherapy. I feel angry at a country that has produced so many depressives and yet doesn't seem to have begun to address the problem. Who do I talk to about it? I am so helplessly unknowledgeable about norms of care, avenues of approach, possible procedures. But *something* has to be done.

I am thinking particularly of a woman I visited a couple of weeks ago, but not for the first time. She lives with her family, three generations of farming people, though she sometimes goes into the hospital's psychiatric unit. Usually we talk in the sitting room, with other people in and out. But this time she wasn't feeling very well so I was shown into her bedroom. She sat in a chair, almost silent at first, but gradually getting out a few words. And then a few more. We were getting somewhere. And then she drew back. Something she didn't want to talk about. I was fairly sure I knew what sort of thing it was. But no, she went back into silence. Her husband brought tea in for us and joined us and that was that.

The next day I rang the hospital and asked to speak to the head of the psychiatric unit. I told him who I was and outlined the situation. I asked if she was getting psychotherapy when she was in there. And was shocked by his brusque reply. 'We don't do that American nonsense here,' he said.

October 18 – Friday

Go to see Sally, to discuss parish music. She was most encouraging and knowledgeable about new music for churches. After seeing her I was suddenly overcome with gratitude for all the good and competent and hardworking people we have here. Like Jenny, and Rose, who are so efficient and reliable, and put in so much work on behalf of the parish. And the churchwardens and glebewardens, who can be counted on not only to do something when it needs doing, but to be the people who notice in the first place that it needs doing. And the ever-faithful Nan, who regularly plays for both Sunday morning services when the other organist is away, without a hint of complaint even though I know she does not find it easy; and who miraculously turned up with an electronic keyboard when the organ of the famine church was dismantled for repair; and whose post office is often the scene of an impromptu parish meeting. And the wonderful Ken, who so quietly chauffeurs people to hospital appointments and looks after them in his gentle way. And so many others, so good, so kind. Truly this place is close to heaven.

October 21 – Monday

Walked down to church at 8.00 am this morning to say Morning Prayer, for the first time since nearly five weeks ago when I tore a ligament under my knee. Have been going everywhere by car ever since, as far as possible. It was good to get the deep breathing of an early morning walk in sea air again.

October 23 – Wednesday

Rosie is in a panic yesterday because she realised, while Richie was still out at sea, that he has several symptoms of TB: an abrupt loss of weight, copious night sweats, and the sort of cough you might expect from a long-term smoker – only, he doesn't smoke. He came in late yesterday and they went to see Dr Larry this morning. He was sent straight to Bantry hospital for an Xray. The technician who took it wasn't qualified to read it but thinks it looks alright. Richie is also to have a blood test next Sunday, by which time he will have had a proper report on the x-ray.

Neither he nor Rosie, it seems, were inoculated against TB in childhood. Rosie was away from school the day her year had them, and we were then told that she couldn't have an individual one and that it wasn't really necessary anymore. I don't know why Richie never had one.

October 24 – Thursday

The other side of the wonder of its still being light at 11.00 pm in June is that now, even by mid-October it is still dark when I get up at 7.00 pm. This morning when I set out for church at five minutes to eight there was still no sign of the dawn light on the ridge of rock behind the church.

October 25 – Friday

… but this morning the light, when I came out of church at a quarter to nine, was astounding. The view across the bay was of leaden pink clouds to the south-east, but ahead to the south-west the sky was a cerulean blue with high white pillar clouds, the blue reflected startlingly in the edges of the flat streams of water coursing across the strand; and everything sharp and clear.

November 10 – Monday

Richie's tests are all clear, thank God. But it's good that it was all dealt with so promptly.

My workload is growing fast, with sorting out parish finances, installing ramps and loop systems and new noticeboards and shelves. And – wonderful – there will be Quiet Days at the beautiful far west church in the summer. And I am gradually persuading people that it's alright to take more part in the services. And there will be as much liturgical and musical improvements as possible.

The annual parish dinner-dance on Friday was a great event. As people traditionally invite their friends and neighbours it was far from being an all Church of Ireland occasion: half the peninsula seemed to be there. And oh! the strange two-step waltzes, and the wild Irish dances, like nothing we had ever seen before. And the energy …! Even from the old people. We left at midnight but were told it usually goes on until three in the morning. I believe it.

November 12 – Wednesday

After weeks of mild weather, and one or two days of its being not so mild, today has been rather cold. I even wore gloves, briefly, for starting to drive the car: but took them off when I got into the village. And never bothered to do my coat up at all. 'Isn't it *bitter*? asked Mary in the bookshop. 'It is a bit cold, ' I agreed. 'A *bit*? This is real winter now.' I was amazed. Apparently it doesn't ever get any colder than this. I went home and almost threw out all my winter boots, scarves, gloves … What bliss to think I will never need them.

One of our parishioners who had been to Cork for a few days was telling me, in a very long and chatty phone conversation how delighted her Catholic friend had been to see in the service sheet of the Church of Ireland cathedral there that 'communicant members of any Christian denomination' were welcome to receive Holy Communion. I tried to say that similar sentiments were expressed on our own service sheets here, but M., who is a dear but much better at talking than listening, was rushing on with 'I think that's wonderful. It means that no matter whether you're a Catholic or a Buddhist or whatever, you can still receive.' I halted her at that point just enough to explain that Buddhists weren't actually Christians. I think she heard. I'm not sure. She has kindly volunteered to be a Sunday School teacher if we can get it going. It is endlessly possible to overestimate how much people know about the basics. I think I just might do a series of sermons on them.

November 13 – Thursday

Beautiful day, mild and deliciously sunny.

November 14 – Friday

Another *beautiful* day. We had lunch out in the garden. A fresh clear blue sky, with real cotton wool clouds here and there. The busy lizzies and the nicotiana are still flowering.

November 15 – Saturday

It's odd how people here sometimes have names that are very old-fashioned but now also new-fashioned. Wilfred, for someone in his forties. Hilda, for a young woman not yet twenty. At first it disconcerts an outsider, a 'blow-in'. But then it intrigues. It turns the whole question of names being in or out of fashion quite upside down.

November 19 – Wednesday

We learnt on Sunday that two of our parishioners have just been up to Dublin to receive their award from Bord Failte, the Tourist Board, for the Best Farm Guest House in all Ireland. I had been going to ask them to book us a few rooms for some of the guests at Rosie and Richie's wedding next June, so I made a joke about being sure they were now fully booked for the whole of next year and they laughed and agreed. Today I learnt it was only a joke. I can of course have some rooms next June: but Violet wouldn't hear of taking a booking yet. Bookings don't start coming in until March or April, she said. Even when you're the best farm guest house in all Ireland … ? The joke about the Irish, that the word *mañana* expresses far too much urgency, doesn't do justice to them. The point is that in Ireland *mañana* is an exceedingly long way off.

November 27 – Thursday

Matthew arrived at Cork Airport with a little bag and a big bag. All his worldly goods. He has come to live here. Which is both lovely – and slightly scary. We had almost become accustomed, John and I, to being parents-at-a-distance, with our four boys in England and Wales, and only Rosie here with us – and she now primarily in another relationship. But Matt has no other relationship – it will shift family dynamics interestingly.

November 28 – Friday

The day's mail has brought notification from the County Council of proposed road closures for horse trotting races over the Christmas period. The first one is on Sunday December 15 from 1.00 pm to 5.00 pm, along the road our church is on in the town. At 3.00 pm that day we have our carol service there. Ecumenical. 'Ah, so the people of all denominations get kicked equally,' says the delighted man I speak to at the County Council offices. 'No discrimination. That's grand.' We have a very jolly chat, ending with his saying I should leave it with him and he'll speak to the organisers. The last time they had an objection, he said, was when our tiny hospital on the same road said it couldn't be held in case they might suddenly need to do major heart surgery.

That call to the County Council started with my getting a pleasant woman telling me I had a wrong number. But the number was the one in the phone book, I said, 37258 for the County Council.

'Ah, I know. But the number you need is 21299,' she said. She was right.

The road where the horse trotting races are held

November 30 – Sunday

Good to be able to have the Advent hymns. I haven't heard any Christmas carols in the shops yet. Maybe they start later here – that would be good too.

December 5 – Friday

In the hairdresser's in the little town a great conversation gets going, a four-way chat through the mirrors: two of us swathed in miscellaneous cloths (who needs colour-co-ordinated décor *here*?) and Ann the hairdresser, at different stages of curling (Elizabeth) or cutting (me); plus someone I don't know who pops in for a chat. The peat fire in the little grate is nice on this sparkly cold day, but Ann is bothered that her supply of peat briquettes is low. 'I'll have to ring Tom' (the owner of one of the two mini-supermarkets down the road) 'and get him to bring me up a few,' she says. And he does.

December – 15 Sunday

If this is winter I think it's wonderful. It is so *uncold*. Today, for example, after church, everyone was saying that it is very cold, yet I am walking about with no gloves on. Me, who used to wear gloves (fingerless) not just to church but in church as well for most of the winter in Norwich.

Yes of course it rains quite a bit: but many days are blue-skied and clear. The landscape is beautiful in a different way now. With foliage gone you can see through things and around things, see the shapes of trees and rocks, and lanes and farmyards that you couldn't even guess at in the summer. Houses you didn't even know were there.

In the garden nicotiana is still flowering, and Chinese lilies, and marigolds.

December 16 – Monday

Road racing is like nothing I have ever seen before. I think what is done here is properly called trotting races, or harness races. The jockey doesn't ride the horse: the horse pulls the jockey in a 'sulky', a very light-weight two-wheeled cart. From Main Street, all down the side street that our town church is on, the paths were packed with onlookers. So packed, in fact, that some of the pedestrians were on the roadway. Which seemed horribly dangerous when the horses came racing through us, metal hooves thundering on asphalt, two or three at a time down the not very wide road. Sometimes the horse's feet skittered but they never actually lost their balance. Even though I knew some of the many participants, including at least one parishioner, I've no idea who won. No matter, it was quite an experience. And the weather was kind, and the enjoyment of the onlookers was great.

December 24 – Tuesday

There has been a murder, yesterday, just a couple of miles from here. A French woman visitor found battered to death in a lane near her holiday home. Everyone seems stunned. And tomorrow is Christmas Day. It is not going to be good.

December 27 – Friday

I underestimated the effect the murder would have on our Christmas celebrations here. It's almost as if everyone is stunned frozen. In our Christmas Day services in the two churches the congregations seemed just to whisper the responses. And could hardly sing the carols at all. Betty tells me that what is behind it all is not only fear for the lives of themselves and others but that the murderer will turn out to be someone they know, one of them.

Winter 1997

January 6 – Monday

The horrific murder of Sophie Toscan du Plantier has pulled the whole area into something like a mass depression. Some don't want to talk about it at all, but some are full of speculation, fuelled by the newspapers. The murdered woman was a French film producer who had a holiday home a few miles from us. Her badly beaten body, in her night clothes, was found in the lane by a neighbour.

January 10 – Friday to January 13 – Monday

To Belfast, to conduct a retreat for the women of the Columbanus Community of Reconciliation. They were kind and good and radical and holy, but I let them down, didn't do it well, was too tired after all the rush of Christmas. Which I said, at the end, and they understood and were even more kind. The train journey from Dublin into Belfast had been unexpectedly terminated at Portadown because of a bomb scare. After a delay, the bored passengers were taken into Belfast by bus. This was my first experience of Northern Ireland, and a revelation. Just from the physical state of the place I got a feeling of harshness, of – how can I say this? – of a masculinity that makes the South feel feminine.

On my second day there, having a free afternoon, I walked around the local streets, and on impulse went into a corner shop for a packet of Polos. And gave the man behind the counter a coin from my pocket. Just too late I realised I hadn't brought any British currency. The man practically flung the coin back at me. 'I can't take that,' he spat – yes, he really did – 'that's *Irish*!'

The journey back to the South reminded me of the train journey from prison to home eleven years ago: freedom, relief, elation, adrenalin. Words and words poured into my head, but I had only a tiny scrap of paper to write on. Which I here transcribe:

County Down: small little deep hills that roll and hummock. Dundalk, Drogheda: softer buildings, Irish language on signs. Back into comfort. Plunging towards Dublin, and a grey sun breaks through. (Oh, *pathetic fallacy*!) Gormanstown: railway by the sea; old boat, half drowned. Then goalposts by the sea, allotments by the sea. Dublin. Home.

February 7 – Friday

Just back from a diocesan clergy conference. A really good couple of days. They are such a lovely lot. I feel invigorated, and hopeful. And rested. And happy.

February 10 – Monday

Ian Bailey has been arrested in connection with the murder of Sophie Toscan du Plantier. John came back from shopping with this news, at midday, having heard it from Kenny, one of Richie's friends, who had seen Ian being taken away by a great number of gardaí. Ian is an English journalist, living locally. He frequents the local bars, and is slightly known by John and me, and well known to Rosie, Richie and Matthew. Matt said that just the other day Ian had been going on and on about the murder, until Matt asked him to stop it.

The early afternoon television news said simply that a man had been detained for questioning at 10.45 this morning, near our town-village. Late afternoon: the news says a woman has been arrested as well as the man. We assume that is his partner, a woman we like, a good artist.

February 11 – Tuesday

The man and the woman were released after the statutory twelve hours that they could be held for questioning. We were right that the woman is Ian's partner. Everybody is now talking about the murder – but with a sort of vitality that has been absent before. It is almost as if the general depression has lifted at the possibility of it being solved. There is already a wealth of gossip circulating about why Ian is a suspect: people who know things, people who saw things. And an assumption that he will be re-arrested in a week or so.

February 12 – Ash Wednesday

A small number turned up today for the service of Holy Communion with Imposition of Ashes. There is no tradition of extra events during Lent, so I will have to put it all into the sermons. No tradition either of not having flowers or greenery in the churches during the Lenten weeks. At least we'll do Good Friday properly, with a full three-hour long service. And I might try for something special for Maundy Thursday.

February 15 – Saturday

Richie has been out at sea for several days, and therefore not here for St Valentine's Day. But Rosie reports he has just got back and has got a card for her – made from the back pages of the Marine Safety Handbook.

February 17 – Monday

On Friday an elderly parishioner I was visiting at his remote cottage handed me a lumpily wrapped package which turned out to be a wad of five pound notes, totalling £700. Today I was given an envelope with £300 in cash in it. Many of the older people – especially, I think, the farmers – are accustomed at this time of year to handing in enough money to constitute their entire giving to the church for twelve months. These two offerings were from people who do not live in any sort of luxury – far from it. I am amazed, and very moved.

February 18 – Tuesday

Terrific gales these last few days – and more expected tonight. Glad Richie is safely ashore. Today, bright

Stormy weather

skies and large hail stones. While I was teaching at the Community College today one of the students came in with a snowball he had made by pressing hailstones together. Very excited, despite his thirteen years. The kids here almost never experience enough snow to make even a small little (as they say here) snowball.

John is taking proper Irish classes in a class run by the College teacher of Irish. I can't because of conflicting work. I envy him: but it is clearly very difficult.

February 19 – Wednesday

I made 27 house calls today between noon and 5.30 pm. Not all the people were home, though perhaps because of the bad weather, most were. They don't count as 'visits' because I was taking around the vestrymen (*sic*) slips that everyone has to sign each year if they want to be considered members of the Church of Ireland. And they can't vote at the Easter Vestry meeting if they don't. That's the theory. In practice, nobody has signed any papers for a number of years, and many are confused by them. The name 'vestryman' doesn't help, as it gives no indication of its function. Maybe it did a hundred years ago. 'Voter' or 'elector' would be better.

I have asked a colleague what the difference is between the parish census that we took last June, and this record of vestrymen. He says the parish census is done every three years and is conducted by the Diocesan Council to establish the size of the parish under certain criteria. These criteria are then used to assist the diocesan Finance Committee to set the 'Assessment' or 'Fair Share' for each parish. The categories are: churchgoing parishioners under 18, churchgoing parishioners over 18, non-churchgoing parishioners under 18, non-churchgoing parishioners over 18, parishioners over 18 away from home at college, and parishioners in nursing homes. So I can see that the list of parishioners who want to be able to vote at the annual Vestry meeting at Eastertide would be different from the parish census – and smaller.

Anyway, notice has been given for several weeks now that these vestrymen forms had to be in by tomorrow. Three people voluntarily produced them last Sunday: the rest ignored them. So three of us have been rushing around the parish getting them signed. Sally and Bill saw all the existing parishioners in the area around the town, and I did the rest of the peninsula today. Well, most of it. A few remain to be done tomorrow (fairly hopeless).

It did at least get me over some thresholds I had not previously been invited to cross. If the poverty I see were part of a film set I suspect there would be some disbelief that twentieth century people in this part of the world live like that. But the people living in them do not seem discontented.

In one house I went to three of the four eligible signatories were sitting in the kitchen when I came in. I'd never seen any of them before. Certainly not in church. The youngest of them, a woman in her thirties, took a form and wrote her name where I showed her to put it, and then signed with the same printed letters. She then took the other three forms and proceeded to fill out one for her husband, one for her mother, one for her brother; signing all of them with their own names. I thanked her, thanked them all. If the others couldn't write, okay.

February 20 – Thursday

The Rural Dean's annual inspection today. We met up in the town, the Rural Dean and two men who were between them architect, surveyor and builder; and one of our glebewardens and me. From the east end of the parish we worked westwards through three churches, two parish halls and the Rectory. And at each church we were joined by one of its two churchwardens. It was all very relaxed. An English Rural Dean would probably have conniptions at the way it is done here. The churches have no written record of their furnishings or silver plate, though plenty of people know exactly what is there, and who gave it, and when ... We had a coffee break at the Rectory midway, and I had been instructed to arrange the tour so that it ended at the harbour village at the end of the peninsula at lunch time. There is a pleasant bar there that looks out over the water. It does splendid food and drink, and is run by Angela, a lovely parishioner – and harmonium player.

February 23 – Sunday

John and I had a good break on Friday. I had to go to Cork for various work-related things on Friday, so we had lunch there, at Isaacs' – marvellous! And when all my work was done we booked into a hotel in the centre of town, and had a small dinner at another restaurant, with food almost as good as Isaacs' but a bit more expensive. Then we went to see a John Cleese film, which was not wonderful but it was such fun to be in a cinema again, with other people, and looking up at a big screen. I've missed that so much these past nine months.

The next morning we did some food shopping in the indoor market, then drove north to Mallow for coffee and then west to Killarney and around through the lakes down to Kenmare, where we had an enjoyable lunch. Then over the beautiful Caha mountains and down to Bantry.

We got back to our town-village just in time for the 3.00 pm lecture on the Famine that we wanted to hear. That was part of the annual Meithal weekend. 'Meithal' (pronounced 'me-hal') means something like 'pulling together in hard times, the urge to co-operate for the common good' and goes back a long way, especially in farming. Most of the events of the weekend take place in the Community College, but the bars also have special music nights, and tonight the closing event is a concert in our church, with the Orlando String Quartet from Holland.

February 25 – Tuesday

Was *en route* to Cork late yesterday afternoon, for a meeting of Diocesan Council, when the car's brake lining pads went, very suddenly. All well when I left home: an hour later, at Clonakilty, they had reached an embarrassingly shrieking stage. Fortunately I found a repair garage at about five minutes to six. They were very good, and set straight away to change the pads. The odd thing is that those same two pads had been replaced just about three weeks ago, and in fact only one of the two was worn, though seriously worn. Something is wrong, and the car will have to go back to our local man this week for him to look at it. This is the first time we've had any trouble with this car, a Ford Fiesta – not bad for nearly nine years old. – I was only a few minutes late for the Diocesan Council meeting.

February 28 – Friday

I was in town without a coat on today. Beautifully sunny. But the sea still too rough for the boats to go out.

March 1 – Saturday

To Youghal, a town an hour the other side of Cork city, for a Franciscan Tertiary's day today. I'm not one, but my dear friend Lesley is, and is so good about inviting me to such things that I said ages ago that I'd like to be there. Stayed overnight with her friends, at the old ferryman's house on the River Blackwater. The river separates the counties of Cork and Waterford. The house is on low land at the very edge of the water and on a curve of the river, so that to stand at the small wall outside the house in the grey morning among the wind and waves is to feel as if you are in the prow of a boat in wild midstream.

Youghal church is very beautiful: the best I have seen in Ireland. Of course, for historical reasons, just about all the ancient churches belong to the Church of Ireland. I almost envy Peter, the Rector there. But it seems it is almost impossible to heat the building effectively. And anyway the town of Youghal, though much touted in the tourist guides, isn't a patch on our own small town. And the landscape around it is rather flat and featureless. I'm so very grateful for where we are.

March 5 – Wednesday

With the encouragement of Peter the Rector of Youghal who is Diocesan Information Officer I have handed out, at yesterday's diocesan 'Clerical' meeting, or posted where necessary, a letter to all the clergy of the diocese saying how valuable I had found the clergy conference last month, but asking if there was a need for an occasional 'keeping-in-touch' paper between these annual events.

March 6 – Thursday

Went today to call on a couple who have lately written me a couple of angry but polite letters. They are early-middle-aged Irish, not churchgoers now, but were once very active in the parish until their favourite church, the one in the middle of the peninsula, was closed down four or five years ago. They were among the first people I visited when I was new here and of course I had hoped that since their quarrel was with the previous Rector they might begin to come to church again. To my knowledge they had never been to a normal service of worship in my time, though they did come to one of the Christmas carol services.

His first letter, written after he had been invited to sign the form saying he was a member of the Church of Ireland, was full of irritation at my using the sign of the cross at the blessing at the end of the Communion service: and he had heard that we were now using wafers instead of the (squashy, plastic) bread that is usual here; and he wouldn't be a member of an organisation that, with under 200 members, installed their 'chairman' (me) in a mansion. In my reply I said I had some sympathy with that last point.

But I was intrigued that his second letter, responding, was a litany of all the dreadful things that the clergy had done to him. So when I visited them today I asked whether he thought the clergy is the church, or whether the people are. The clergy, he said unabashed. To my mind, I said, clergy come and go, and the real church is the lay people who are there forever – he shook his head fiercely – and was he not aware, I went on, of all the lay people in the parish who had expressed great sadness at their having stopped coming to church, and maybe he felt some obligation towards *them*? It didn't move him. 'The Church' has done this, 'the Church' has done that, it was changing everything and that was all wrong, it was not the way they were brought up, etc., etc.

There is much anger in him, seeking targets everywhere. I felt sorry for him. He's a good man, I like him, and I like his loyal wife also. We went on to have a lively and enjoyable talk that ran well over my usual hour. Yet I don't see any way, apart from prayer, of moving towards reconciliation.

March 13 – Thursday

It is dreadful news that Mary Robinson is not going to stand for re-election as President. Is Ireland's great day over? She has *been* the new Ireland.

Have had quite a lot of good response to the 'touch paper' I sent to the diocesan clergy.

March 15 – Saturday

A few weeks ago the Bishop asked me to tell him when I was likely to be in Cork so that he and I and the Diocesan Secretary, could have a talk about a possible information pack for clergy new to the diocese, especially if they are new to the Church of Ireland. There are now three of us here who have recently moved over from the Church of England. As the installation of the new Dean of Cork was to be held in the cathedral yesterday evening, I said I would come up for the day.

In some ways the meeting was good: it was friendly and relaxed and although I worried that the list of possible contents that I had drawn up on the word processor and printed out would be seen as English-ly over-organised, they went through it with me quite amiably. I had suggested a pack to the Bishop a while back. When I was new here I had found it so difficult to get basic information to do with the diocese, including organisations, and regulations, and who to contact for various things, and how things are done, and where to get things and so on. So we talked about the possible contents of such a clergy information pack. I couldn't tell if they were for it or not.

But right at the end of the meeting we got onto some of the unfinished business of the recent clergy conference, including the monthly *Diocesan Magazine* – whether it should be changed – and the national weekly *Church of Ireland Gazette.* As editor, in my former life, of two diocesan publications I felt able to express an opinion. I am convinced that the layout of the *Magazine*, which is in effect a series of parish newsletters, one after another in alphabetical order, could be changed to good effect. With its present format I'm sure most people read little more than their own parish news – which in some cases will appear identically in their parish newsletter. The *Gazette* is like something that might have been produced a hundred years ago. Surely only a completely new publication would do. (I trust I put it a little less bluntly than that.) Yet the Bishop and the Diocesan Secretary defended them both and appear to see no need whatever for change. Of course I've no idea what diocesan or national or personal politics lies behind their not wanting to agree with me.

They told me there had been a survey of the *Magazine*'s readers a few years ago and ninety-five percent had said they like it as it is. I suggested as tactfully as I could that as they had never experienced anything different it was hardly a meaningful vote. Of the *Gazette* they said that it was wonderful that, with part-time staff and no money or resources, it had survived so long. When I listed some of the many Irish church events that were reported in the Church of England weekly *Church Times* but never mentioned in the *Gazette*, like the award to the Corrymeela Community, or the financial rescue of the Irish School of Ecumenics, the Bishop said that really nobody here would be interested in those things. I said the *Gazette* hadn't even mentioned that Religious Education was going to become an exam subject in Irish schools, and showed the piece about it by Gregg Ryan in the *Church Times*. Ah well, I was told, Gregg Ryan was a professional journalist who needed to turn out whatever stories he could.

It's all very depressing. Do I give up and cultivate the garden – or fight and make a whole load of enemies? Interestingly, at one point the Bishop said something about XY, an archdeacon in one of the Church of Ireland dioceses. I met him at a gathering in England at a time when I was sorting out whether I should or could work here, and he was very encouraging. Last year he was spoken of as a candidate for Archbishop of Dublin, before Walton Empey was chosen; and it has intrigued me that his name did not come up again in speculation about the two new episcopal vacancies that have occurred since then. But now I know why. 'He's seen by his own diocese as a high flyer,' the Bishop said. 'The Church of Ireland doesn't like people who push themselves.' He admitted that that was hard on XY, as circumstances have pushed him, rather than he himself. But I wondered all the same if it was a warning to me: don't push. It's probably too late already. The 'touch paper' of which I sent the Bishop a copy for his information, is probably wildly pushy. What the heck.

The installation of Michael Jackson as the new Dean of Cork was on balance an enjoyable event. I was reminded of the first time I was present for a big service in Cork Cathedral back in June, when I was so depressed by the way it was all done that I fled, tea-less, as soon as it was over. This time I stayed for tea. Was it marginally better – or have I become acclimatised? I suspect the latter. The organ was too loud, the choir mostly inaudible above it; the congregation stood for far too long, and determinedly remained facing forward when the new Dean was led to the back of the cathedral to be 'given' the font. The congregation was, according to the service sheet, meant to sing the psalm with the choir, but couldn't and didn't. And the ceremonial greeting of the new Dean by specific members of the congregation and the community was effected invisibly and apparently in total silence.

But it was almost all redeemed for me by the fact that the preacher was Rowan Williams, Bishop of Monmouth. His address was simple and short and good to my ears, being based on St Patrick's 'I bind unto myself today the strong name of the Trinity.' Afterwards at the tea I went over to Rowan, whom I had known years ago through the peace movement and the contemplative prayer groups I had started. I got a hug from him and a great chat about his new baby, and about the Church in Wales' first ordinations of women and what that has meant for him: a chat that left me both warm and desolate. It brought home to me all the clerical energy and shared goals that are present in the British clergy at its best. When I said my habitual words of enthusiasm about being here I sensed from Rowan just the slightest raising of eyebrows.

Those two parts of the day have firmed up something in my mind. I like being in Ireland. *Is maith liom í.* No, I love being in Ireland: *is brea liom í.* But at the moment I am not very keen on the Church of Ireland. Oh.

Later: The implications of this have been going round in my mind ever since then. I can't help wondering, what am I doing here? What drew me here was the sense that somehow, with my long enthusiasm for ecumenism, I had something to offer in a country where it had seemed possible that the Catholic Church and the Anglican Church might be drawing closer together. I didn't know if it was my involvement in the wonderfully ecumenical prayer groups – nearly 400 of them in the UK – or my concern for communications that might help things along, perhaps with a new ecumenical newspaper; or simply by being here and encouraging it all at the grassroots. Yet not only do all those once promisingly ajar doors now seem to be shut, but I am beginning to realise that anything I try to do is going to be hampered by my being seen to be English. Which actually I am not. Irish mother, Welsh father. But I speak with an English accent. I have an English passion for getting things organised. *Ergo …*

If God had a hand in my coming here, as I believe God did, then it wasn't for the reasons I thought. I love my parish. I love my parishioners. I will be content with being where I am, able to do what I do.

March 16 – Sunday

Elizabeth A. came into the vestry before the service began and told me that Patrick, one of the local fishermen, was drowned last night. He had gone out alone, as usual, to spread his nets, and had not come back. They sent out a search party when he didn't appear in his usual place in Kitty Newman's bar. His body was brought in this morning at 8.00 am. We remembered him in the prayers. Most people had known him.

March 17 – Monday

St Patrick's Day. With lots of prior notice, and encouraged by the Irish language teacher at the Community College, we said the Lord's Prayer in Irish at Holy Communion this morning at *Teampol na mBoct*. I think we did very well, as not many can speak Irish. Someone pointed out that it was very appropriate in that building as those who built it during the famine would have been Irish speaking.

A good crowd this evening at the local drama group's production of George Bernard Shaw's *You Never Can Tell*. But it was odd to hear those extravagantly English lines spoken in most cases with Irish accents.

March 18 – Wednesday

Matthew has been doing some amazing work on the land between the Rectory garden and the higher, wilder land that lies beyond that. We have been told that the Rectory land is, in all, thirty-three acres, most of it rock and gorse, but also a plantation of pine trees. The part that Matt is

*The back gate of the Rectory (top) and
Rectory garden (below)*

working on consists mostly of small trees, too close for any grass to grow, on uneven levels of bare soil, and with a small thin stream wandering through it. He is creating a circular walk, starting from the right hand corner of the end of the lawn and re-emerging at the left hand corner. The more he works the more sure he is that there was once a formal garden there, and at one side, an orchard. He has found edgings where flower beds must have been, and roses now wild, and rather tumbled remains of some stone steps. It took John and me nearly twenty minutes to do the complete walk.

And to one side of all this, at the side of a slightly bigger stream, are the clear 'lazy bed' ridges of the remains of a potato bed. The Revd Mr Fisher's vegetable garden, that we were told about when we first came here!

March 26 – Wednesday

Beautiful sunny day for my birthday. John and I had lunch in the Courtyard in the town-village, and were joined by Matthew and Rosie. Richie is out at sea. I took the afternoon off.

As we were about to leave the town some workmen who are refitting one of the bars in the main street – well, they are all in the main street – brought a very long roll of carpet out of the building and hauled it right across the street and set it down. They then proceeded to untape it and roll it out along the road; then twisted it ninety degrees and rolled it up again. A big truck was about to come down the street but stopped. Gradually a few other cars stopped behind it; and then traffic from the other direction also stopped. In all it took about five minutes.

Nobody seemed to mind about being held up. After all, it was a nice day.

March 28 – Good Friday

Yesterday we had a Holy Communion service combined with a Passover Seder – all taking place around a long table in the town church, with chairs and a tablecloth and glasses and plates. It was totally new to twelve of the thirteen people who attended (Sylvia had been to a Seder-Communion in England last year). And with two exceptions they took to it without any apparent misgivings. I find that very encouraging. Even though only that number chose to take part in it, at least it means there is a solid core of people who are not scared of doing something they've never done before. And they did seem to get a lot out of it, in terms of understanding-through-doing the origins of the Eucharist, of re-living the Last Supper. And they combined with great ease the desired informality and reverence. Afterwards they kept thanking me for having arranged it.

The two exceptions were a couple of retired farmers, man and wife, who were visibly disconcerted by the form of the service, even though I had explained last Sunday what it would be like. They are good people, and I was sorry for them. I must go and see them.

Today we had the Three Hours, from noon until 3.00 pm. Passion readings and prayers and hymns, and a lot of silence in between. People come and go quietly for whatever amount of time they wish to spend there. One dear woman stayed for the whole three hours.

Nan told me last week that in past years it was the tradition to go on Good Friday to one of the strands at the end of the peninsula to dig for cockles. She remembers from her youth the crowds of people who used to go. And she thought probably a few still do. Apparently there are some very low tides at this time of year.

March 30 – Easter Day

Today was disappointing. I remember I was disappointed by our Christmas services and wondered if the people here are just not very good at celebrating in a church building. Then someone said to me that it was because of the local murder, two days before, that everyone was very subdued. But that doesn't apply today. Again there was a general inability to raise any sort of sense of celebration. Maybe I didn't do my part very well? John asks if it is because the Church of Ireland people are *dour*? I don't think it's that, it's not true of the people themselves, although I admit to seeing the Church of Ireland's liturgical sense as dour, and its buildings as sometimes rather grim. But the people themselves, at the annual dinner dance for example, are very capable of enjoying themselves. No, it feels more as if they are scared to let go into joyousness in a church building. Reverence yes, celebration no. I expect it goes back into history.

But I have Easter home Communions to do. Fourteen of them, including two couples. Plus however many there will be at the town hospital: probably three or four. The visits can be spread over a few days. That will be good to do.

Spring 1997

April 2 – Wednesday

The tourist season of requests to see the registers is beginning again. I usually put people in the dining room with the registers spread out before them and I leave them to it but hover about, and often they do find the records of ancestors that they were looking for. Yesterday there were two Americans from Washington DC. Today, a very shy man was asking for a copy of his entry in the register of baptisms, and a 'letter of freedom', to say that he is free to marry. This happens when a non-Roman Catholic wants to marry a Catholic.

I had never seen him before, though his parents used to be on our parish lists. 'Have you ever been married before?' I asked. 'No,' he said. He seemed too shy to be other than honest. So I typed out 'To Whom It May Concern – To the best of my knowledge ABC has never been married before.' I suppose if I had been doubtful I would have checked with the churchwardens or anyone who has lived here all their life. The last 'letter of freedom' I had to write was for another putative parishioner a year ago who wanted to marry a Filipino woman living in another country. He had met her a couple of times. I wrote the letter, he moved to that other country and is back here again I understand – on his own. Sad.

Putting the registers away yesterday, my eye was caught by an odd bit of spelling. At a wedding here in 1851 the clergyman has written the bride's surname as 'Splaine'. In the signatures – and they *are* signatures not just 'X, her mark' as so many of them are – the bride signs her name as 'Spilane'. It wasn't just in Shakespeare's time that there was a freedom of spelling for surnames!

I called on the farming couple who had been so disconcerted by the seder on Maundy Thursday. Only the wife was home. 'No, we didn't like it,' she said. 'We didn't like it at all. *He* wanted to leave but I said you can't do that, not in the House of God. But we didn't like it. We like the *proper* Maundy Thursday service like Canon __ used to do.' She was quite amiable about it all but very firm in telling me how they felt. She also said that 'a lot of people' were leaving because they didn't like the way things were done now. I said they should tell me what they didn't like, not just leave, because that didn't change anything; but telling me might. The services were too long, she said, people needed to get home to cook their dinner.

All this was said so civilly and without rancour that I went away mildly depressed, wondering about all these people who were leaving, nearly a year after my arrival. Later I saw Nan and Betty, two of the Nominators who had selected me as their next Rector. I asked them if they thought people were leaving. They were surprised. No, they said, if anything the numbers were going up. Ah, but they weren't I said: attendance numbers in the registers were down on last year's. I shan't repeat what they said but it seems I should not pay too much attention to past statistics.

April 7 – Monday

The hedgerows are lavishly scattered with violets. I have never seen so many.

April 8 – Tuesday

Easter Vestry (the annual church meeting). It was a good meeting, very good I thought. We made a break in the middle of the usual formalities of an Easter Vestry meeting, after the reports and before the elections, to have a brain-storming-and-buzz-groups session about what is good about our parish and what might be better, and how. More people attended than in previous years, apparently, because I had been making a real appeal to the congregations to treat it as our one chance to have an annual meeting of the whole parish, and to *be* there. People were talking really animatedly in their separate groups, so that the plenary session that followed was very constructive. It was even suggested, after someone complained politely about the communion wafers I've introduced, that we use matzot, as being nicer plus more authentic! All in all, it was very encouraging.

April 9 to 13 – Holiday

Our first trip back to England since moving to Ireland a year ago. Hectic, because we were trying to see forty different people or couples or households in twenty days. But enjoyable. Seeing people – family or friends – and often staying with them for one night or two, was a more heightened and precious experience than simply knowing them used to be. But then it was sad leaving them.

When we got back home we went house hunting, because our large three-storey, five-bedroom, terrace house close to the centre of Norwich had finally sold. We went to our friend Jim, the estate agent in the town-village, and asked what he had on his books for the amount that was now in our bank. Nothing, he said, not for that price. Everything he mentioned was out of our reach. We were almost out of the door when he said, rather dubiously, that there was one small cottage … a holiday cottage, really … about a mile out of the town. We went to look at it. A traditional stone building in a couple of acres, at the foot of what the local people call 'the mountain.' Like a child's drawing of a house: a door in the middle, a window either side, and three windows upstairs. A chimney at either end. Whitewashed, and standing in long grass. One long room downstairs, one long room upstairs. A bathroom tacked onto the back. A stone shed nearby. We loved it all. And are negotiating to buy it for our retirement. And until then a home for Rosie and Richie after their wedding.

The house we bought for our retirement

May 8 – Thursday

William Qammaniq, the Inuit boy injured here last summer, is dead. He died in hospital in Montreal, having never really regained consciousness. Sad, sad, sad. His father Johnny has been at his bedside – first in Cork, then in Montreal – ever since he and Nancy arrived from Canada a few days after the accident. How will it be for him, going back to what used to be his normal life?

May 20 – Tuesday

Only a month now to Rosie and Richie's wedding. Rosie is very organised about it, which is fortunate because it is all going to be done on a shoestring.

Richie is lovely. The other day Matt was depressed. John and I sat around trying to talk him through it and out of it. Then Richie came along and, seeing how things were, simply took Matt out for a drive all around the peninsula. Matt came home again quite revitalised and full of the sights he had seen. Depression vanquished. Brilliant.

May 23 – Friday

Last week I took some holiday leave and went to Scotland on Tuesday, to lead a Quiet Day for a contemplative prayer group there on Wednesday. Enjoyed it enormously: the travel (leisurely connections), the landscape of Dumphries & Galloway, the lovely people and the very kindly hospitality, and the utter silences of the Quiet Day in this very quiet corner of Scotland.

May 24 – Saturday

An elderly American friend has just stayed overnight with us. Driving him back to Cork, I mentioned that I needed to stop for petrol. 'You still call it petrol?' he asked in surprise. I was amused by the unstated assumption that by now we should have grown up into calling it 'gas'.

May 25 – Sunday

Yesterday was John's and my 40th wedding anniversary. A Saturday, fortunately, so we were able to have a lazy morning and then go into the town-village for coffee in the Courtyard, then to the local horticulturalist for some colour to fill spaces in the huge long garden. Back to the town for a pub lunch, and home after doing the

Celebrating our fortieth wedding anniversary

shopping. One elderly parishioner had rather chided me in the Courtyard for being in jeans and an open-necked red shirt. 'I don't recognise you without your collar on,' she said.

In the afternoon Rosie and Richie came round with a surprise, a wonderful bird table for the garden; and then began preparing supper for us. It was a great meal and altogether a lovely day. We had cards and phone calls, and John and I wore the long origami paper necklaces that Mary my former Parish Worker had made and sent us: hundreds of multicoloured, folded paper birds.

May 27 – Tuesday

Yesterday I had to take the parish photocopier into Cork to be repaired again. And had a meeting of the Diocesan Council in the evening. So Rosie and I spent the afternoon doing 'wedding shopping.' A *lovely* day. Weather perfect: totally blue sky, temperature around eighty degrees but with a breeze. We had lunch at the Gingerbread House, supper at the Quay Co-op. Shopped separately to begin with, then met up at 4.00 pm at Maguire's for a shoes-off, tired-feet-on-stool, drink. Real mother-and-daughter stuff. Great. Rosie now loves Cork, feels at home in it.

May 28 – Wednesday

To Charles Fenn's ninetieth birthday party yesterday evening. Charles was a photographer with AP (Associated Press) and a BBC correspondent, becoming a specialist on the subject of China and Vietnam. His book on Ho Chi Min (1973) was a classic of its time. He and his wife came to our town in the 1970s when it was a shabby little fishing village.

We gathered in his house on the edge of the harbour and, after a kiss and a hug and a chat with Charles, talked with the other twenty or so guests, and enjoyed the champagne buffet prepared by his artist daughter Alyn. Later, the Vanbrugh Quartet, who until then had been ordinary members of the party, found their instruments and played for us: Mendelssohn and Smetana, Charles's choice. Outside the large glass window the sun went down over the harbour, lighting the room, the company, the music. What privilege to be part of such a happy evening.

The town harbour

May 31 – Saturday

Twenty-seven degrees centigrade at nine o'clock this morning when I took my late, lazy, day-off breakfast out into the garden. It's been another amazingly beautiful day, warm and sunny yet with a slight breeze. Now, at five in the afternoon, the thermometer stills shows thirty one degrees. And this is Ireland, which we were told was never cold in winter nor hot in summer.

Later: someone was saying to me that our garden must be very warm because it is so protected by the rocks and the trees. Then, on the News, we heard that West Cork has been experiencing a record twenty-seven degrees. Our garden beats that!

We went out at lunch time today to the cottage, the one we are buying for Rosie and Richie to live in until I retire. We wanted to show it to Richie's cousin and occasional employer, who is a builder. We need an estimate for redoing the roof. After he'd gone John and I walked further up the mountainside, up a track that was sometimes pure rock, past a sort of small empty and overgrown house and then a ruined cottage – and found the Council's concrete water tank in the field beyond. The estate agent had told us that the water supply for the cottage comes down from the water tank through rubber pipes laid into the ditches.

June 7 – Saturday

Last week we got some fascinating information. We have been shown the 1901 census for the area in which 'our' cottage is, and found it because we know that the same family, who moved out of it only fairly recently, were there since it was built about a hundred years ago. Three of their descendants are still parishioners of ours. There they were. All of one family name. It seems that there were three older people there, and ten people between the ages of five and 24. Doing a bit of guessing, Joseph, a man of 60, listed as 'farmer', was married to Ellen, a woman of 48, also 'farmer'. Three females, Lizzie, Mary and Eva, aged 15, 16, and 19, were listed as F.'s daughters and two males, Frank and Joseph, aged 17 and 24, were given as F.'s sons. But there was no F. Away from home at that time? Or deceased perhaps. Ursula, aged 50, was probably F.'s wife. The names of four other children, Richard, Thomas, Sarah and George, aged eight, 12, 13, and 14, were followed by the word 'scholar'. But of the littlest one of all, Ursula, aged five, it was said she was a scholar, but couldn't read! Only one of the adults, farmer Joseph, could not read.

It looks as if Ursula and the absent F. had five children, all of whom they chose to list as F.'s sons and daughters. And Joseph and Ellen had five children, whom they listed as 'scholars'.

So thirteen people were living in 'our' small cottage? Perhaps some of them were in the small stone building near the cottage. And there are ruins of another building slightly to the north of the cottage.

Ten years later, in the 1911 census, only seven people remain. Ursula, presumably widowed, is 65, and her son Joseph, 34, is a farmer. Ellen and Joseph are now 59 and 73 (?), both still described as farmers. Their sons Thomas and Richard, now 20 (?) and 18, are still living there. Their daughter Ursula is now 15 and can presumably now read.

June 9 – Monday

We have just had our big parish weekend com-memorating the building of *Teampol na mBoct* – The Church of the Poor – 150 years ago during the Great Famine.

On the Saturday afternoon in the church we had a lecture on the famine in this peninsula, given by the County Reference Librarian. That was followed by tea at the Rectory for all who came to the lecture – all seventy-two of them? Probably: the tea pouring seemed endless! We now have some good little booklets for sale about the Revd Mr Fisher and the Famine, that John and Rosie have produced with help from Nan. And some beautiful tea-

Hilary in Teampol na mBoct (photo by John Minihan)

towels, designed by a parishioner's daughter and based on a drawing from that time.

Then in the evening, also in the church, there was a recital, with organ, violin, cellos, piano, and children's choir. Only thirty-two came to that. I don't know why musical events are so poorly attended here. Some are excellent, others less so, but the audiences are always pathetically small.

Then yesterday, Sunday, the Bishop came to celebrate our parish Communion service, and preach about the anniversary. Very good sermon, and a very good service altogether, people seemed to think. The church was comfortably packed, though I couldn't help noticing the people who weren't there who I think should have been. Some are still angry with the Bishop over the closing, five years ago, of what was the fourth church in this parish. Others presumably wouldn't come because it wasn't *their* church. This service had been heavily touted as a whole-parish event, and there was no service in either of the other churches that day. But long years ago this parish was three or four parishes. Persuading the parishioners that they are now one parish is still apparently hard work. And some of the local people, I suspect, don't want to have to do with anything that refers to the famine because in this area that brings up the still terrible issue of souperism. For that reason, the Catholic parish priest of this part of the peninsula had said apologetically a while back that I shouldn't ask him to take any part in this 150th anniversary.

Bishop Roy is a good man. And I like Mrs Bishop too, she's very gutsy. After the service they joined forty-two of us for lunch at one of our local hotels, and that was very enjoyable. So now everyone is saying what a good weekend it was.

The Bishop said an incredible thing when we were waiting in the vestry before the service began. We were talking about relationships between the churches, and he said that when he was a curate, forty years ago in Northern Ireland, there were two criteria for a sermon. One was that it had to be well-peppered with biblical quotations – 'even if they weren't relevant to what you were saying!' – and the other was that it had to include a swipe at the Roman Catholic Church. Incredible.

June 10 – Tuesday

Wedding preparations have taken over our house – and our lives – for the past week or two. This is going to be a very homemade wedding. Rosie spends most days in the Rectory kitchen, making and freezing mountains of quiches, dips, and savoury pastries. Lists proliferate, pinned up on walls and stashed in folders. I am so grateful that Rosie is doing just about all the catering. I've had to tell her she is not being allowed to set foot in the kitchen on the day itself or she will arrive at the altar a haggard exhausted creature. I have little still to do apart from arranging to borrow things like trays and large platters, and promises of garden flowers, and getting the parish hot water urn, plus cups and saucers, from the parish hall to here; and making some minor alterations to her dress, which was bought second hand as their wedding gift by her brother Tully and his wife Angie in England. I finished their wedding present quilt quite a few days ago: they are reassuringly pleased with it. (As I am too.)

One worry is that the water supply to the Rectory will give out on the day. The water table is very low, despite recent rain. I've never heard of anyone wanting to turn wine into water, but it could happen …

June 12 – Thursday

The first Quiet Day at the bare-stone church at the end of the peninsula. Taken by Fathr Benedict Moran, OP,

Prior of St Dominic's Montenotte, Cork. At my request he gave three addresses on *Lectio Divina,* a meditative way of reading scripture. Only six other people turned up (I think we can publicise better next time) but it was a very good day. That church is the perfect place for a Quiet Day: spartanly simple and so beautiful, surrounded by a grassy graveyard and rocks and uneven grazing land. And the harbour on one side and the sea on the other.

June 15 – Sunday

Rosie and Richie have given John an old dinghy (called here a punt) that was Richie's, complete with outboard motor. John is over the moon. Best present he has ever had, he says. It is moored in the bay at the end of our avenue.

June 19 – Thursday

The whole community is being so kind about this wedding. John went to the agricultural co-op for petrol a day or two ago, and was asked how things were going. He mentioned the water problem. They all started thinking of solutions. 'We could wash out our molasses tanker for you ...' 'The Council have tankers – have you asked Michael?' And came up with the fact that Peter H., a local farmer, would probably have a large tanker free. When John told me this I said I knew Peter and Eileen, as I had baptised their third child recently. First John rang the Council, who said we could have water from them but they didn't have a spare tanker. Then I rang Eileen. Thinking that if they could let us borrow a tanker I wasn't sure how we'd get it the five miles or so from the farm to the Rectory. Eileen said they had a water tanker but they use it for the cows.. 'But we have a large milk tanker,' she said. 'It's the sort you can get into, to clean. I'll clean it out for you. When do you want it? Do you want the Council's water, or ours? If it's for drinking, you don't want it standing too long: we'll bring it over to you on Saturday evening. No problem. Any time.' Of course we invited them to the wedding, but no, they thought that with three small children they wouldn't. Amazing, wonderful.

All week people have been fixing things up: friends of Rosie and Richie have put up a huge blue tarpaulin from the back door of the Rectory to the doorless garage, where the bar is going to be. The little hotel in the town-village has lent us tables and chairs and glasses and trays, and Richie's father Johnnie has been collecting them all. The Courtyard bar has lent us more glasses. Tom at the village supermarket has given us a load of ice to chill the 'champagne' and hinted at extra foodstuffs on the day. A couple of parishioners have given us a carload of beautiful arum lilies for the church, after watering and watering them for a week or more to ensure they were in the best condition; and other parishioners have lent us freezer space, and sets of garden chairs and tables, and even an extra freezer; and have brought loads of flowers for the house. Others will be involved in arranging the church flowers, and taking part in the service in various ways. And my dear Nan will be playing the organ.

The presents that have been pouring in are just fantastic. Richie and Rosie now have more cut glass, lead crystal, than I have ever seen outside a shop: all from members of the community, Catholics and Protestants and others. My parishioners tend to give practical things: a coffee maker, a food processor, a sandwich toaster, a dinner service. Nan brought some crochet work back from her holiday in the Aran Islands. The shopkeepers have given wildly extravagant presents from their stock: one of them just reached down the largest stainless steel saucepan on the shelves and gave it to John to give to them. And there have been presents from the doctor, the vet, and the gardaí.

Rosie says women she hardly knows are coming up to her in the street and hugging her and wishing her well.

June 20 – Friday

Richie's uncle, Father Connie, has arrived on holiday from Nigeria to help me marry them. He seemed surprised that I wanted him to share the service with

The arrival of Richie's uncle Father Connie

me, although I had said that from the very beginning. Of course, if it had been in the Catholic Church, as first planned, he or the Parish Priest would have done most of the service, with me just reading a prayer or something. That's how it is usually done. But I think that in a mixed marriage the service should be as fully shared as is ecclesiastically allowed.

Our family and friends are all piling in. With only (!) three spare rooms we can only have closest family staying here at the Rectory, but others are in a rented cottage and various local B&Bs and hotels. They report that the whole community is talking about the wedding. My sister-in-law, Pat, has made a magnificent wedding cake, four tiers high. My mother has paid for the service sheets. Our London friend, Judy, has done some fantastic flower arranging in the house – like in our coal hod, and in an old paint-smeared galvanised bucket. And is to do Rosie's garland and bouquet tomorrow.

Tomorrow. The day.

June 24 – Tuesday

It was wonderful. Nothing went wrong, everything was lovely. Loads of friends and family, calm and organised, helped with the final preparations in the morning, so that the house was all ready by the time I went down to the church just before 2.30 pm.

The bride's mother is supposed to cry. I supposed I should have when the bride arrived because she looked so beautiful. I did get slightly choked at the end of the address/homily, looking down from the pulpit at the two of them and saying their names. The service went

Groom, bride and mother of the bride

smoothly I think. There was a startling amount of clergy: not just Father Connie and me, but a priest-colleague of Connie's, who just turned up and was introduced to me; and the Parish Priest also, who had been invited at the last minute, but *sin scéal eile* – that's another story. All up in the tiny space around the altar, they were.

And afterwards Liam the fiddler led us from the church the short distance along the road and up the avenue to the Rectory garden, playing a traditional Irish wedding jig. When the crowd was all into the yard the cake was cut and the glasses of bubbly were taken around and the speeches were *very* nicely made and the cake was distributed and everyone was talking to everyone.

The cake was cut ...

... the band set up to play ...

A while later we called people into the house in a one-way system, for the buffet meal, which Richie had embellished at the last minute with three huge lobsters; and then the bar was opened. And a bit later the musicians settled down to play. As it began to get dusky some people began to dance. So there were the musicians, sitting under the blue, blue tarpaulin, next to the shiny water tanker, playing excellent Irish music, and sometimes singing; and there were people dancing, at first on the concrete area but then as more joined in, out into the yard.

On the other side of the tanker there was the bar, nicely contained in the cleared-out stone garage that Richie had white-washed months ago. And all around the grassy part of the yard there were tables and chairs in great circles – no, horseshoes – of observers and chatterers. Our friend

... and the dancing began

Tony has made a willow arch, with a flower wreath at each end, over the stone gateway into the garden, and some people went through it onto the long lawn. A few people were in the house, where there was still food, and where John had lit a fire in the drawing room. But mostly, the yard was the place. It was such a good feeling to be moving around and talking, and drinking, among such a very mixed crowd of people.

As it got a little darker, and the older people left, one of Richie and Rosie's friends made a small fire in the middle of the yard, for the bride and groom to jump over. The glow of it, and the softening of voices, was magic. It was of course Midsummer's Night. It never really got properly dark. Even when the band stopped at midnight it was only gently night-like.

And so many people said afterwards that it was the best wedding they had ever been to. Because it was homely, they said, not like the rather formal ones, going off to receptions in hotels. And there were cautious references to the mixture of people, and somebody said if only some of the Catholics and Protestants from the North could see this …

And Richie and Rosie were so good, and looked so happy. It is a joy that they have found each other; and strange to think of the way things have happened since our coming here just over a year ago.

Eventually everyone went home. There had been no fights, no breakages, no nastiness. Everyone had been so together, and gentle, and kind, and happy. It was a wonderful, wonderful day.

Afterword

IT IS TWENTY-FIVE YEARS now since I became the rector of that parish. And twenty years since I retired early on health grounds in 2001. John and I moved to the foot of the 'mountain', to the little cottage we had bought for retirement, and Rosie and Richie and their wonderful baby, Cian, moved from there to a flat in the next village. Later they moved back to a house in the town-village.

John had in 1999 started the poetry magazine THE SHOp, whose patron was to be Seamus Heaney. I joined him as co-editor when I retired. As we were still living in the parish I dutifully stayed away from church services for two years, going to other churches in the area, to give space to the new rector, Eithne. And then came back as a parishioner, although with Permission to Officiate (PtO) in the diocese. By 2017 John had serious mobility problems and we moved back to England, to Norwich, where he died in 2018. I am now a parishioner (with PtO) in the parish where I had been vicar before we moved to Ireland.

Twenty-five years ago, when this diary started, the Republic of Ireland was a very different place from what it is now. Already, funds from the EU were improving the roads and other amenities. **Then from the** mid-1990s to the late 2000s **a period of rapid growth,** the 'Celtic Tiger', took over the economy. That Saturday in May '96 when at nine o'clock in the morning I drove fifteen miles to the nearest big town, and passed only one other vehicle, is almost unimaginable now. I did that same trip experimentally recently and stopped counting the cars and vans and trucks after I passed seventeen of them. Ireland has changed so much. The newspapers and church magazines that seemed fifty years out of date then, in the 1990s, are totally changed now: lively and colourful, and available online.

There are some other loose ends that I want to tie up.

There have been several changes of Rector in the parish since I retired in 2001. And the Parish Priest, Father Hurley, died at a sadly early age.

Attempts by the French authorities to extradite Ian Bailey, the British man who is the only suspect in the murder of Sophie Toscan du Plantier, have so far failed, though many hearings have been held in Ireland. Our Rosie and Richie have been key witnesses. *The Irish Times* has reported: 'Ms S... testified along with her husband Richard at Ian Bailey's libel action in 2003 that they believed he was confessing to the killing when he broke down on New Year's Eve 1998 and said to them "I did it, I did it, I went too far." '

That trip I made to Northern Ireland in January '97, with the unpleasant incident that put me right off the place, has since been followed by many more, to Belfast and Armagh, to Newry and County Down, for poetry and religious events, and all were very pleasant and full of good people.

The head of the hospital psychiatric unit who, when I asked him if they provided psychotherapy, said, 'We don't do that American nonsense here,' was later succeeded by a really splendid head of psychiatry, Dr Patrick Bracken, who has only recently retired.

The Heritage Centre in the former church building in the middle of the peninsula, now houses sail makers and menders.

Hairdresser Ann moved from her little cottage shop, with its cosy fireplace, down Main Street to an elegant salon, where I would still go any day for a haircut and her company.

Religious education has become an examination subject in Irish schools and now has qualified teachers.

Some of the ecumenical contemplative prayer groups that I had hoped would start in Ireland, the Julian Meetings, (see May 18 '96 and September 16) did eventually happen, about five or six in all, from Northern Ireland to Dublin to this southwest corner. But I think only one still exists, and that in the North. I guess the Irish don't really enjoy silence very much!

We never did find the ghost we had been told was in the wild acres behind the Rectory.

Our beloved Rosie, who had been ill for some years, died at Cork University Hospital on December 9, 2019. Richie, and their son Cian, still live in that town-village, and are still very much a part of the family.